Um Kamal

MOTHER OF KAMAL

To Mary,

with best wishes

Fawzi

Um-Kamal

MOTHER OF KAMAL

FAWZI IBRAHIM

Published by KFI Publishing Ltd, London

All characters and events in this publication, other than those clearly in the public domain, are fictitious and any resemblance to real persons, living or dead, is purely coincidental.

First published in 2022 unless otherwise stated

A CIP record of this book is available from the British Library.

Cover: iStockphoto

Printed in England

ISBN 978-1-3999-2305-7

For my mother, Um-Jamil

1

1952 – Aqrah, northern Iraq

IT WASN'T UNTIL the last turn in the long road that hugged the mountain range for miles that he saw his destination, the small village of Aqrah, a region of the Duhok Governorate of Iraqi Kurdistan, where the houses sank into the mountain side, one row above the other, the roof of one forming the front yard of the one above. For the want of paint they could be described as picturesque. On the other side of the valley, elegant mountain goats perched high up on the vertical mountain face, with no obvious means of support. The sky was pale blue, the air fresh and pure, the sun bright and hot, and a white-tailed eagle effortlessly and majestically floated high up in the sky. It circled the village. The car door opened, and Kamal popped out into the market place, glad to be able to stretch his legs after the two-hour bumpy and, sometimes, hair-raising journey.

The market place boasted a baker, a butcher and a café, where men sat holding small, delicate glass cups between their forefingers and thumbs, sipping chai. The 'hee-haws' of a donkey, who had it in mind to bray continuously, competed with the voice of Um-Kulthum singing one of her marathon songs, relayed from Cairo via an old short-wave radio powered by a large car battery. At the far end of the market square was a spring. Crystal-clear, ice-cold water spouted out of a perfectly formed hole in the rock face.

The white-tailed eagle, spying an easy meal, swooped down onto the meat display at the butcher's shop, scattering dust and flies in all directions. It sank its sharp claws into the best part of half a lamb's carcass, spread its formidable wings, and tried to take off; but with little room to flap its wings to generate the necessary thrust, and the heavy load in its talons, coupled with the beatings it was receiving from the butcher's besom broom, a dignified exit was not on the cards. White, red and brown feathers floated across the square. The eagle lent on its left wing and, using it as an extra limb, pushed itself up, furiously flapping the other wing in an attempt to extricate itself. In this endeavour, the bird was inadvertently helped by the butcher swinging his broom up and down, sweeping air underneath the beast, and so increasing the thrust. With one colossal downward sweep of its wings, followed by another, the eagle crossed the threshold necessary for take-off and flew across the market square. It was just high enough to avoid the heads of the men sipping tea, but not the large turban of a startled man sucking a melon. Two boys, in their early teens, gave chase; but the eagle with its dignity now intact and self-respect restored, and with the white fat of the lamb glistening in the sun, took a left turn towards the deep valley and, aided by its thermal currents, the magnificent creature soared away, and soon was invisible to the eye.

The café owner came over to welcome the new arrival, his broad smile betraying two missing front teeth.

'He wants to know what business you are in,' interpreted the driver.

'I'm the doctor,' came Kamal's reply. '*El-Duktor*; your new doctor.'

For a moment, everything in the market went quiet – even the donkey stopped braying, and Um-Kulthum was in the middle of one of her signature long pauses. Everyone stared at Kamal. Immediately a short sturdy man, wearing flimsy brown slippers, took hold of the doctor's hard-shell trunk, lifted one end, carefully slid underneath it and, by bending his knees, pressed his back against it. He stretched his arms over his head and, in a well-practised manoeuvre, simultaneously pulled the trunk forward by its leather strap and straightened his legs. He had the large trunk, twice his weight, perfectly balanced on his back; and, without a single word, and with his arms outstretched to help his balance, he walked steadily up the mountain track. Kamal followed, wondering if this was heaven or hell.

The porter dropped the heavy trunk on the stone floor of the small courtyard and looked at Kamal. Kamal, not used to such situations, embarrassedly searched his pocket for some change and gave him whatever he happened to find, which was far more generous than he had intended. The porter took a quick look at what he had been given, clasped the coins tightly in his right hand, afraid they might be taken away from him, and lifted his arm to touch the forehead of his slightly bowed head, murmuring something that Kamal took to be 'God bless you', or something similar. The porter walked backwards a couple of steps, turned around, and left.

The square courtyard was in semi-darkness, with the only light coming from the narrow doorway. Kamal looked around at what was going to be his home for the foreseeable future; the only doctor serving a large district with a population of thousands, not far from the Turkish border, in a semi-isolated Kurdish area, where feudal traditions prevailed.

The courtyard had a kitchen area on the left, with an oil stove and a water tap – the only water tap in the house. There were two doors and an arched passageway. One door led to a sparse bedroom, the other to an equally sparse lounge with one settee, two armchairs and a medium-sized oak dinner table with three chairs. A chicken seemed to have made itself comfortable on one of the armchairs, though it noisily departed when Kamal stepped into the room. The passageway led to another, slightly larger courtyard which, going by the wooden benches that were arranged against the wall, was obviously a waiting room for would-be patients. A door at the far end of this courtyard led to the surgery, with a small wooden table and two chairs. Another door led to a storeroom-cum-pharmacy with several shelves holding large bottles containing various compounds, acids, and other assorted chemical substances and medicines. There was a set of balance scales and a variety of small weights on a large table. Kamal didn't know why, but everything looked eerily familiar. The clinic was built on part of a stable housing the hardy mules used extensively for transporting people and goods across the harsh mountain terrains, and the stench of manure was emanating from the remaining part of the stable at the back of the clinic. It suddenly dawned on him that this was the clinic that the English professor who lectured on public health took the final year students to visit, as an example of the worst type of public health provision. A strong sense of apprehension gripped his whole body, reminiscent of the trepidation he had felt when he was in that prison cell some five years ago. This was not a posting; it was a punishment.

'*Duktor!*' said a tall man in an immaculate uniform who exuded authority. 'The door was open.' He stretched out his right arm, giving Kamal a powerful handshake that lasted longer than was comfortable.

'*Marhaba, ahlan wa sahlan*, welcome,' he continued. 'Masud Aslani. Did they give you a proper welcome at the market place?'

'Well, yes,' said Kamal, astonished at how the tall man seemed to feel at home in the surroundings. 'Someone carried my trunk on his back all the way up the mountain track, without me even having to ask. He moved so fast, I had a job keeping up with him.'

'Yeah, that will be Aziz, the porter. And you gave him far more money than you should. Must be careful, people will take advantage of you.'

The man sat on the armchair that looked least likely to have been inhabited by any domestic or wild creature, and drawing out every syllable, as if to properly be understood, he said, 'AB… RA… HAM… You are of the Jewish faith. Is that why they sent you here Doctor?'

'Your guess is as good as mine.'

'Either that or you killed someone. The last doctor raped a nurse, and they wanted him out of the way. How long do you think you'll be staying with us Doctor?'

'It's not in my hands.'

The man continued, without paying attention to Kamal's answer. 'The last doctor was here for six months. He bribed someone and was released from his contract.'

He took a Turkish cigarette out of his pocket, lit it, inhaled deeply, and exhaled, watching the smoke spread out towards the window and, as if talking to himself, said, 'I've a feeling you'll be with us for a long time.'

'I'd offer you a cup of chai,' said Kamal, 'but I don't know where everything is.'

'No need. When will you open the clinic?'

'Tomorrow, I assume.'

'*Wallah!* Really? That soon? Normally, doctors wait for a week or so before they take their first patient.'

'The sooner, the better. I have nothing else to do.'

'Abu-Rahman will be here first thing in the morning. Anything you want, just ask him.'

'Abu-Rahman?'

'Yeah, the caretaker. He knows everything. He'll also translate for you. Most of the people come from remote mountain villages, and they only speak Kurdish.'

The man stretched out his arm and shook Kamal's hand, with the same ferocity as before. 'Very glad you're here, Doctor. Don't hesitate to contact me if you need anything.'

'How can I contact you?'

'Just ask for the Chief of Police.'

He walked out to the courtyard towards the door. 'I'll get someone to bring you some food. I'm afraid it won't be kosher,' he said, as he turned to leave. 'And don't give him more than 3 fils, otherwise they'll think you're made of money.'

Kamal smiled to himself. Not that long ago, Kamal had been arrested by the police; today he was being courted by them.

2

Baghdad – four years earlier

TWO WEEKS HAVE passed since martial law was declared. Hundreds of individuals, communists, intellectuals, teachers, refinery workers, journalists and students have been arrested. Stories abound of people being taken away for no other reason than the way they look, speak or behave. Three people were hanged in the main square and left there as a warning. Lists of those sentenced to prison appear in the newspapers every morning. There are tales of beatings and torture in Abu Ghraib prison.

The knock on the door startled Reina but, at the same time, she had been expecting it. It was the police; an officer in plain clothes, with a small moustache and wire spectacles resting on a large nose, and two sidekicks in ill-fitting, coarse, khaki-brown uniforms with handguns in holsters on their hips.

Reina gingerly opened the door.

'Where are they?'

'There is nobody here. I'm on my own, leave me alone.'

The officer pushed the door open, forcing Reina to fall back against the wall of the washroom beside the door, as he stepped into the small stone courtyard.

'Search the house for the Jewish vermin,' ordered the officer.

'I'm a woman, on my own,' pleaded Reina, as she pulled her abaya tighter around her shoulders. 'Where is your respect? You're a Muslim, you should respect your elders. I'm old enough to be your mother.'

'My mother wouldn't have criminals as sons, let alone Jewish criminals,' replied the officer, looking at his sidekicks with evident self-satisfaction.

Hearing the commotion, two of Reina's wanted sons, Kamal and Sasson, suddenly appeared and a brief, futile, scuffle ensued.

'Tie them up,' ordered the plain-clothed officer, punching Kamal on the left eye and Sasson on the chin. 'So, you want to overthrow the government, you filthy Jews.'

Looking at a crumpled document in his hand, the officer said, 'You have another son, Ezra. He is to come with us too.'

Ezra, who was reading in the first-floor bedroom he shared with his two brothers, realized the danger and sneaked out. With careful steps, he reached the staircase and fled to the roof. The pigeons, on seeing him, started to coo in anticipation of some food. He took out a handful of seeds from a sack and splashed them in their direction to keep them quiet. Then he jumped over a narrow gap to land on the roof of the neighbouring house and disappeared.

The plain-clothed officer ordered a search – which was an excuse for rummaging and smashing their way through the house, throwing things on the floor and breaking anything that didn't move. They found neither Ezra nor anything incriminating.

Reina, who was also known as Um-Kamal, or mother of Kamal, after the custom of naming the parents after their first son, pleaded, 'Take me instead, they've done nothing.'

'Done nothing? Conspiring to overthrow the government and kill the King is doing nothing?' screamed the officer, as he gestured to the two policemen to take the two brothers away.

'Nana, don't worry, we'll be alright,' said Sasson.

She looked at Kamal, who, though the older of the two, looked more frightened than his younger brother, and reassured him, 'Don't be afraid. I'll make sure you are out soon.'

The plain-clothed officer shoved a folded piece of paper into Um-Kamal's hand and then followed after his two sidekicks, who were taking turns in beating the two brothers.

She unfolded the paper and stared at it. It didn't make any sense to her as she couldn't read. The only thing she could recognize was the red and blue stamp of the dreaded *al-Mukhabarat* on the top right-hand corner. She had never regretted her illiteracy more thanshe did in that instant. She'd always remembered with regret the moment her parents, who had three daughters to marry off, took her out of school.

* * *

Twelve-year-old Reina was lying in the bed she shared with her two sisters. It was late evening, and the one-room household where the family socialized, cooked, ate and slept was faintly lit by a single candle placed in a pale green pottery holder. Only a few days ago, she and her two sisters had begun basic education in a girls' school that had recently opened. Her husband to be, a young man with prospects, having seen her coming back from school, followed her home, then sent a friend to ask her parents for her hand in marriage. She overheard her parents talking.

'What does she need education for? Why does she need to read and write?' her mother had asked. 'She'll be married and raise children,' said her father.

So the young Reina was happy; she need not go to school in the morning, and she didn't.

* * *

She sat on the stone floor, tears in her eyes, folded paper in hand, waiting for her husband or any of her children to come home to decipher the unfathomable characters on the paper. There has been talk of thousands of arrests, torture, and sentences passed en masse by judges sitting through the night. Her children are good boys, well behaved; they don't fight in the street like so many of their age; they don't steal, or anything. Kamal in his second year in medical school, and Sasson top of the class in Al-Shamash secondary school; why should they be arrested, she asked herself. They'd done nothing wrong; they were considerate and helpful; they cared for people; she was proud of them. Not many parents send their children to school, let alone have any at university – she had two; her eldest daughter, Rosette, and her eldest son, Kamal, both studying medicine. The image of Kamal's frightened face flashed before her. She was not so much worried about the younger son, because she felt he could look after himself; but for her eldest, Kamal, it was a different matter.

How she wished she could read.

Rosette, one of the first women in Iraq to study to be a doctor, came back early from college. Several students and staff had been arrested, including her professor. The lecture on pathology had been cancelled. Rosette looked at the paper that Reina handed her.

'It's just the standard document they give out when they arrest anyone,' she said. 'It says they have taken them to the Central Police Station. Nothing here to say what they are charged with.'

The next day, Um-Kamal was up before sunrise. 'Don't worry,' she said to her husband, Abu-Kamal. He had spoken not a word since he came home to find that two of his sons had been taken away for no reason that he knew of. 'I'll sort it out.'

She left Rosette to ensure that the four younger children went to school and made her way to the Baghdad Central Police Station where a large group of women, all mothers and sisters of those detained by the authorities, dressed in the traditional black abayas, gathered in front of a large gate that was guarded by two stick-wielding policemen, shabbily dressed in khaki uniforms. There were no men. Fathers and brothers would not dare to come for fear of being arrested. There was no queue, and the crowd swayed one way, then the other, like a gentle wave on the shores of the Tigris, as they attempted to get near enough to the gate to grab the attention of the guards, who spent more time smoking and chatting than attempting to bring any semblance of order.

When Um-Kamal managed to get near the front, she found that only two people were allowed in at any one time, and only when the previous two came out. The commotion, pushing and shoving, and the absence of any form of order meant that it was as impossible for those outside to get in as it was for those inside to get out. No one was prepared to give an inch. It was a miracle that anyone managed to get in or out. From time to time, one of the guards would point to one or two women who would be the next to enter the compound. Those who shouted loudest and pleaded hardest seemed to get preference.

After two hours of manoeuvring this way and that, Um-Kamal managed to get inside the gate where, across an unpaved open yard, stood an office. An officer in a clean and tidy uniform sat behind a table with three stacks of papers held down by two heavy stones and half a brick, lest they fly away on the occasional rush of air through a glassless window that was quite unnecessarily open. She showed him the letter from *al-Mukhabarat*. He glanced at it with complete disinterest and handed it back.

'What do you want?'

'My two sons, Kamal and Sasson. Can I see them?'

'They are not here.'

'But the note says they have been brought here.'

'Just because it says they've been brought here, it does not mean they are here.'

'At least look at the list,' said Um-Kamal, pointing to a pile of papers in front of him.

'Listen... what did you say your name was?'

'Um-Kamal.'

'Um-Kamal, this list hasn't been updated for three days.'

He started sifting through the pile of papers in front of him, occasionally wetting his forefinger with saliva to make it easier to turn the pages. 'Kamal and Sasson, you said. Sasson is not a Muslim name. Are you Jewish?'

'Yes.'

'Why didn't you say?'

He picked up another pile of papers and started sifting through them. 'No, I don't have their papers here. Come back tomorrow.'

'Will you know more tomorrow?'

'Come back tomorrow,' he repeated.

As she waited to be let out of the gate, the woman standing next to her said, '"Come back tomorrow"; it's always "come back tomorrow".'

'Is it your son?' asked Um-Kamal.

'Yes, my son, Faisal.' She spat on the ground. 'I named him after the King.'

'What has he done?'

'They say he has been handing out leaflets to workers in the foundry. He can't even read!'

'Was he taken away yesterday?'

'No! Over a week ago. I've been coming here every day, and every day they say "come back tomorrow". I don't know where he is and whether he's alive or dead. He is only twenty.'

The gate suddenly swung open, and they squeezed through a wall of women pressing in the opposite direction, none of whom was prepared to give way lest they lose the tiniest of advantages. After a few minutes, Um-Kamal popped out from the thick wall of abaya-clad women like a cork from a Champagne bottle.

It was midday by the time she made her way back towards home. The sun was high up in the sky and her shadow on the barren ground didn't stretch much beyond her feet. Sparrows, with beaks open so wide one could be forgiven for thinking they had been dislocated, stood panting under the few bushes scattered along the desolate road. She had stopped for a drink at a street vendor, when she heard someone calling her name. It was her niece, Farida, a pleasant woman in her twenties, whose husband came from Um-Saib, a small village 30 or so miles from Baghdad, with a traditional Arab culture, and from where Al-Haddidi, a leading district attorney, also came.

'Go to the attorney's wife, Um-Adnan, and see if she can have a word with her husband,' said Farida. 'They are good people; they know my husband well.'

Two days later, after another 'come-back-tomorrow' visit to the police station, she made her way towards the prosperous part of Baghdad, where roads are lined with tall palm trees crowned with distinctive large hand-shaped leaves, pregnant with bundles of ripening fruit. A gentle, warm, dry desert wind disturbed the finger-like green fruit; brown and yellow dates strewed the pavement. The houses have iron gates with rows of barbed wire stretched along

6-foot-high brick walls, designed to deter even the most determined of intruders. She pulled the handle hard and listened to the ding-dong of a distant bell, which felt like an echo of her beating heart. A dog barked in a menacing manner, and a woman dressed in the traditional abaya walked slowly out of the door towards the gate to let her in. Two Eurasian collard doves resting on a nearby tree took fright as the gate squeaked open.

Um-Adnan was sitting in the open courtyard on a cushion, with a fan in her hand. 'Abu-Adnan is not at home,' she said, when Um-Kamal explained who she was and the purpose of her visit.

'I'll wait, now that I'm here,' said Um-Kamal, who proceeded to clean up the table and sweep away the few brown tree leaves that drifted into the courtyard, finding a home on the marble floor.

'Please, you don't have to do that,' implored Um-Adnan.

'It's okay; I've to do something while I wait.'

The attorney had not returned by the time Um-Kamal had to leave, before her younger children came back from school.

The fruitless visits to the attorney's house became her ritual for the next three days. On the fourth day, a Friday, Um-Kamal left home just when the haunting Muslim call to prayer reverberated all over the city. She went straight to the district attorney's house. It was Friday; he was bound to be at home after the morning prayers. Abu-Adnan was at home. He was entertaining some dignitaries in the lounge, where women were not allowed. The women gathered in a side room chatting and exchanging gossip. Um-Kamal took no notice of Um-Adnan's insistence that she must not disturb the men, and went straight in. A dozen or so men dressed in fine Arab robes sat on luxurious sofas and in large armchairs, smoking nargila, munching fruit and cracking pumpkin seeds. She went straight to the attorney, kneeled down and kissed his feet.

'*Ummi*, mother, *Ummi*, what is the matter?' asked Abu-Adnan.

'I seek your mercy. It is not for me. You can kill me now – but for my two sons. They've done nothing. I implore you, save them.' She kissed his feet again.

'*Ummi, goumi,* get up, there is no need for that,' begged the district attorney. 'Get up. Even if they killed with blood, I'll get them out.' His response echoed his deep cultural roots that went back centuries, which required a man to protect those who seek mercy and treat them as their own. He pleaded with her to get up. '*Goumi, yalla* – in the name of God, get up.'

'May Allah bless you and bless your son and your lovely daughter.'

Abu-Adnan walked to the far corner of the lounge, took a piece of paper from a pile neatly placed on an oak desk and, bending over, began to write. Um-Kamal looked at the guests, who looked back at her in astonishment at her boldness. Abu-Adnan walked back and, handing the letter to Um-Kamal, said, 'Bring me their papers.'

Um-Kamal walked out, saying, 'Thank you, bless you.'

'By the end of the day, you'll see your sons,' Um-Kamal assured her husband when he came back from the early morning trip to the market to get what she had asked him to get. This time she didn't examine what he brought back, or castigate him for the lamb that had little or no fat, or the apples that were too small, or the tomatoes too ripe – a ritual that was played out every morning. This morning, sensing his distress, she told him that his sons will be home today.

'They'll be home today,' she repeated, as much to convince herself as to reassure her husband. Then she left for the Central Police Station, clasping the letter from District Attorney Al-Haddidi close to her breast.

It was dawn, and the air was cold with a hint of humidity. Everything was waiting for the sun to rise and scorch the earth once again, as it did every day. A cockerel decided to call time on the night before. Otherwise, all was quiet till the call for prayer rang out when Um-Kamal was crossing Al-Aimmah Bridge on her way to the police station on the west bank of the Tigris. She was there early, but a crowd of women had already gathered, and professional letter writers had set up their stalls, some with large black Imperial typewriters ready to type letters and appeals for mothers and sisters who were anxious to discover the fate of their sons and brothers. Waving the letter from the District Attorney above her head, Um-Kamal forced her way to the front of the crowd and demanded that the guards let her in. One of the guards held the letter upside down and stared at it. 'Do you really think I'll fall for this?' He attempted to hand it back to Um-Kamal.

'Read it. It is from his Excellency, the Attorney, *Muhami Almuqataea*, Al-Haddidi.'

Passing the letter to the other guard on the other side of the gate, he shouted, 'Hey, Ahmed, what does this say?'

Ahmed, holding the letter the right way up, stared at it at length, and looking up at Um-Kamal said, 'Anyone can scribble this and make out it comes from his Excellency.'

'If you don't let me in, you'll have to answer to his Excellency.'

Other women, sensing a possible victory, albeit a minute one, shouted at the guards to let Um-Kamal in.

The guards eased the gate a little and Um-Kamal, grabbing the letter from Ahmed, squeezed through the narrow gap, without uttering another word.

She went straight to the ramshackle office at the end of the yard.

'Ah, Um-Kamal,' said the officer, 'I've good news for you.'

'And I got a letter from...'

'The good news is I now have the papers for your son, Sasson.' He sifted through a pile of papers and took out a fresh-looking document.

'It says here Sasson got eight years.'

Um-Kamal was devastated. Her earlier energy disappeared as her hopes were dashed. She felt weak and her bones suddenly started to ache.

'And you say it's good news!'

'It could've been ten. Last night's judge gave ten years to everyone, but your son was an exception.'

She paused to catch her breath. 'Can I see him?'

'He's been transferred to Mu'askr al-Washash. We don't keep them here, once they are sentenced.'

'What about his brother?'

'His brother?'

'Kamal.'

'Kamal... Kamal... I have nothing here.'

'But Attorney Al-Haddidi wants to see his papers,' she said, handing him the letter.

He examined the letter, lifted his eyes and looked at her at length. 'Where did you get this?'

'From his Excellency. You can see his signature.'

The officer's face turned pale and, with a slight tremble in his hands, he sifted through another pile of papers and took out a file, from which he extracted an official-looking document. With a fountain pen he began to write slowly and deliberately. When he had finished, he handed the document to Um-Kamal, without saying anything.

'Is he here? Is Kamal here? Can I see him?'

'No visitors are permitted here,' said the officer, and, pointing to the paper, he said, 'Take it and go.'

Seven days after his arrest, Kamal stood outside the Central Police Station. It was early morning and the muezzin had just finished calling the Muslims to morning prayers. To Kamal's left a group of women covered in black abayas gathered outside the main gate. He noticed a woman waving a piece of paper, pressing through the throng. There was some commotion, but he took no notice, his mind being preoccupied by something else.

The sun blurred his sight, and his mind wasn't much clearer. He was reluctant to go home. He picked up a newspaper and turned to page three for the list of the overnight sentences, which filled two whole columns. His name stood out at the very end: FREE. His hands began to shake and his body tremble, as his eyes scanned the page erratically, looking for his younger brother's name: EIGHT YEARS. The words on the page began to blur, as the newsprint absorbed his tears. He was consumed with guilt, and with a need to somehow justify what had happened.

Kamal crossed the Al-Aimmah Bridge, and looked at the fast-moving water of the Tigris, with the round black bitumen *kuphars*, and a couple of rowing boats riding its gentle waves. He concluded that jumping off the bridge would not necessarily result in drowning. He was too good a swimmer, and there were so many boats on the water. He turned towards Rashid Street, and looked up at the glittering golden dome of Al-Kadhimiya Mosque. The large white storks had returned to their stick nests on each side of the central minaret, in perfect symmetry, as they do each year. Summer was well on its way.

The guilt soon began to give way. What happened happened; none of which was his doing. Surely, one son in prison is better than two. He was sure the family would understand; in fact, they must agree it's turned out the best way it could. After all, it's just a matter of luck who gets what sentence, he reasoned. It isn't as if there had been trials!

But it wasn't just luck.

As he approached the house, doubts began to creep in. Best claim ignorance, he thought. The first he heard of his brother's eight years, was when he read of it in the paper, which, of course, was true. What goes on inside a prison cell stays inside a prison cell. It must!

Um-Kamal arrived back home exhausted. Kamal was standing in the small courtyard. She immediately held him in her arms, feeling for bruises and any signs of beatings or torture.

'Did they hurt you?'

'No, they never touched me. They didn't even question me. All of a sudden, this morning, they told me I can go.'

'What about Sasson? Why did he get eight years?'

'I don't know. I've just seen it in the papers.'

'Did he say anything to you?'

'No. They kept us in different cells. I never saw him.'

3

A few weeks later

'He's good. The professor is good,' said Kamal.

Kamal and Sahib sat against the stone wall in a garden space, barren but for a lonely eucalyptus tree in the middle, with a solitary female woodpigeon sheltering amongst its leaves. They munched the unique pita bread known as *samoon*, stuffed with feta cheese and cucumber. It was a short lunch break before they continued their visit to the one mental health facility in Baghdad, *Beit el-Majnoon* – the home for the insane. They were coming to the end of their five-year university course. Soon, they would qualify and be posted as doctors to various regions of the country.

Sahib laughed. 'It was funny how fast *el-majnoon* climbed down the tree. The staff tried everything to lure him. They threatened him, cajoled him and bribed him, but he wouldn't budge. No sooner had the professor pulled a pencil out of his top shirt pocket and moved it across the tree trunk in a cutting motion, than *el-majnoon* hurried down. He was terrified that the professor was going to chop the tree down. He almost broke his leg.'

Reflecting, Kamal said, 'You remember the lecture he gave us on denial?'

Sahib nodded.

'If this episode was repeated every day, say for a year, with the staff looking on in approval, would the professor convince himself that he could actually cut the tree trunk with his pencil?' marvelled Kamal.

'You mean, will self-deception creep in?' said Sahib.

'I read about a case where British prisoners of war in a German camp concocted a scheme to get one of their number sent home by pretending he was suffering from an extreme form of psychosis. He had to keep up the pretence twenty-four hours a day, and they all had to go along with it. Everyone played their part very convincingly – so convincing that the Red Cross persuaded the Germans to let him go back to England on compassionate grounds. When he got home his symptoms continued. They became real, and he never recovered.'

'That's a fascinating story, if true.'

Kamal hesitated.

'I told you about the time when Sasson, my younger brother, and I were taken to Baghdad Central Police Station?'

'Yeah, you were released without charge, but your brother got eight years.'

'But I never told you what actually happened in that place. In fact, I never told anyone.'

Kamal didn't smoke, but he asked Sahib for a cigarette. Sahib put the cigarette he was smoking between his lips, pulled out a packet of Fatima Turkish, took one cigarette out, and handed it to Kamal, striking a matchstick on a stony wall and lighting the cigarette. Kamal inhaled, coughed, and gave it back to Sahib. Sahib laughed, stubbed the lit tip of the cigarette on the ground, and put it back in the brightly coloured packet. The cigarette packet carried a picture of an Ottoman woman wearing a wedding veil, with a Turkish Cross on her left and a red star-and-crescent icon on her right.

'For two years,' continued Kamal, 'I've been saying that we were separated at the police station, that I was kept away from Sasson, and that we never met. But that wasn't true. We were in the same cell, which was completely bare except for a mat made of straw.'

* * *

The cell was damp and the bare floor cold. The only light source was a bare 40-Watt bulb suspended from the ceiling. Any daylight from the narrow opening, high up the north-facing wall, had long vanished. Day by day, the other inmates were taken to the court house 100 yards away, where the Court Martial sat in permanent session. None returned. Now, only four were left in the cell. The two brothers had had their daily half an hour in the yard, and now it was the turn of the other two inmates who shared the small, flea-infested cell.

Sasson and Kamal crouched in the corner on the concrete floor. Each had two cans, one for water and the other for urine. Sasson was still just a sixteen-year-old schoolboy, while Kamal was not much older at twenty-one. This was the first time they had been alone since their arrest six days earlier.

Holding his head in his hands, Kamal said, 'I'll never survive this. I might as well be dead.'

'Pull yourself together. Don't admit to anything. We'll be out in no time,' said Sasson.

'No one's ever come out,' sobbed his older brother. 'We'll never see Baba and Nana again. We'll never see Rosette, Ezra and the kids. My exams, next month; I'll never graduate, never be a doctor. I don't think I can survive even one slap on the face, let alone torture. I'll tell them everything.'

'They have nothing on us.'

'I would rather be dead. I think I'll kill myself – jump out of a window at the first opportunity and end it all...'

Kamal sank to the floor, sobbing. Sasson put his arms around him. He held Kamal's head tight and pressed it against his young chest.

That night, Sasson, lying next to Kamal on the floor, heard his older brother talking in his sleep, trembling, sobbing, crying.

* * *

THE FEMALE WOODPIGEON flew down from the tree and landed on the ground in front of Kamal and his friend, its feathers below its beak ruffled and wet, a sign of a feeding mother. It took a few cautious steps towards the two young men, hoping for a casual crumb or two. The pigeon tilted its small head one way, and then the other, looking at each of the two medical students in turn. It followed the movement of Kamal's fingers as he moved his hand up, and placed the last piece of the *samoon* into his mouth. Realizing there were no crumbs to be had, the pigeon flapped its wings and flew up in to the tree.

'I heard the cell door open late in the night. I'd just managed to get to sleep. I opened my eyes, and in the dim light that floated through the door I saw Sasson being bundled out by a guard. And, before I could say anything, the door was slammed shut. That was the last time I saw him.'

Sahib nodded.

'The next morning,' Kamal continued, 'the same guard came in and said I could go. I said nothing. I got the few things I had, and left. I didn't know that in the early hours of the morning, Sasson was taken in front of a military judge who gave him eight years. I only found that out when I read it in *Al-Sabah*. It was only later that I heard he had confessed.'

'Have you spoken to him since?'

'No, he went straight to Nigret al-Salman.'

'Didn't you go to visit?'

'Are you joking? Ezra, my other brother, did, or tried to. He went all the way to Nigret al-Salman. It took two days. When he got there, he wasn't allowed to see him. He was lucky. He could have been arrested on the spot. Only mothers, sisters and elderly fathers dared visit.'

'Why are you telling me this?'

'When I got out, I was a toxic mixture of emotions – elation and sadness, joy and despair, panic, fear, guilt and, most of all, shame. I decided to say that we were kept in two separate cells, and everyone seemed to accept my version of events.'

Sahib lifted his eyebrows and nodded.

'I want someone to know what actually happened before I myself forget. I'm beginning to find it difficult to tell the difference between what I said and what actually happened. You see, Sahib, my memory is getting hazy. Even as I speak now, I'm not certain of the facts anymore. It's Freud's self-fulfilling fakery, except I'm aware of it.'

'It is a classic case of self-deception, but, in your case, conscious, self induced,' said Sahib. 'I think Freud would call it *wilful self-deception*.'

'That's a contradiction in terms.'

'It is the subconscious that is willing it. The conscious is oblivious to it. Classic! Subconscious wilful self-deception.'

Sahib inhaled on his Fatima cigarette, and, as he exhaled the brownish grey smoke, he said, 'Could it be that you're already in denial?'

'No! If I was, I wouldn't be telling you this.'

'Are you sure?'

'I remember what happened very clearly, as if it happened yesterday. It's as clear as daylight.'

'Isn't that the very essence of denial?'

Kamal and Sahib looked at each other and laughed.

'We'd better go back, we don't want to be late. You know what the Prof is like.'

They stood, swept the bread crumbs off their white shirts, and walked back into the asylum.

The mother woodpigeon looked on from its vantage point. When the two medical students disappeared into the building, it spread its wings, effortlessly glided to the ground, and energetically and systematically relieved the ground of every bread crumb that was left behind.

4

Aqrah – Kamal settles in

KAMAL DIDN'T SLEEP well that first night at the Aqrah clinic, and it wasn't because of the rough bedding. He was used to that. He woke up in the middle of the night, sweating. He may have screamed, he doesn't really know. He had that recurring dream again. He is somewhere; sometimes a place he recognizes, other times a completely strange place, not far from home, and he is trying to find his way back, unable to find his bearings, or find the place from which he knows his way home. Sometimes, a bus doesn't come or a road is closed, or he's barred entrance. He walks through alleyways and corridors, up steps and down staircases, and when he finds something he recognizes, it turns out to be not what he thought it was. Sometimes he goes around in circles, and, at other times, he ends up in a vast, open, empty space. He is frustrated and anxious. He knows his mother is waiting and worrying. No matter how hard he tries, he can't find his way home. He wakes up, sweating and out of breath, with a hole in his stomach, perturbed and full of forebodings.

He put it down to homesickness.

Abu-Rahman is dressed in the distinctive traditional Kurdish outfit of light-brown baggy pants, a short, tight velvet jacket over a striped shirt, and a sash that goes around the waist, with a keffiyeh, a turban, wrapped around the head. A thirty-something man, with the demeanour of someone who is used to being in charge, he had come early this morning. His wife, with a basket full of meat, fruit and vegetables precariously, but expertly, balanced on her head, a jug of milk in her right hand, and a cask of oil in her left, followed a few steps behind.

'Good morning, *Duktor*,' said Abu-Rahman, when Kamal popped his head out of the bedroom door, wondering what all the commotion was about. 'Did you have a good journey, *Duktor?*' Then, without pausing for an answer, 'Did you sleep well?'

Kamal opened his mouth to answer, but Abu-Rahman continued, 'Don't worry about anything, we'll take care of everything, and make your stay very comfortable, very comfortable indeed.' He handed Kamal some tea in a delicate glass cup and an equally delicate saucer. 'My wife, Fariza, will prepare some breakfast,' and, pointing to the sitting room, he said, 'Here, sit down, sit down; we'll take care of everything.'

Kamal took the cup and saucer and sat down at the dinner table. He blew gently across the top to cool the tea and began to sip it gently.

'The word is that you want to open the clinic today. Is that wise? No one expects you to do that.'

'I want to make a start.'

'If it's what you want, you're *el-Duktor*.'

He looked at his Swiss Omega luminous-dial wrist watch and said, 'Let's see. It's now eight-thirty. We'll open at ten, and if you are quick, we can finish by noon.'

Kamal nodded.

'Then, you can have your private consultancy at two. You're going to have a private practice, aren't you?'

Kamal nodded.

'That's settled. I'll arrange everything while you have your breakfast. My wife cooks a very good breakfast you know; and her dinners are the talk of the whole of Kurdistan.'

A woman with a young baby was the first patient to come into the consulting room. She had large blue eyes, a bright round face and wore the traditional white head scarf, with a long brown dress and a blue vest. The baby, tightly swaddled, as is the custom in most parts of the Middle East, was whimpering with obvious discomfort. The woman sat on the chair opposite Kamal, her face showing the deep anxiety of a mother whose child is in extreme discomfort and pain. She spoke to Abu-Rahman, gesturing with her hand excitedly, pointing to the baby's belly, touching his forehead, while trying to comfort him at the same time. The baby continued to cry. Abu-Rahman asked her some questions, which to Kamal seemed more like an interrogation than investigation. Kamal waited patiently, alternately looking at the woman and Abu-Rahman. Finally, Abu-Rahman spoke. 'She says her baby has a tummy ache. I told her she was wasting your time. She can't come running here every time the baby cries. I said you'll give her."

The doctor leaned forward and touched the baby's face. It was boiling hot. 'Tell her to unwrap the baby.'

'*Duktor*, it's normal for these babies to have stomach problems. Shepherds' wives, they are simple people, they don't know how to feed their babies.'

Kamal gestured with his head towards the mother. Abu-Rahman, bewildered, sharply instructed the mother to unwrap her baby. The mother started to remove the cotton sheet that was wound around the baby several times. There were traces of blood among the urine stains. Kamal took out his stethoscope, shoved the earpieces into his ears, placed the disc resonator on one side of the baby's tiny chest, then the other side, and listened to the sounds the little tummy was making. He then took a medical thermometer and inserted it into the baby's rectum, and while waiting for the thermometer to register the baby's temperature, he felt the racing pulse. He took the thermometer out. It read 110. Looking at the colour of the urine, Kamal immediately knew what it was. He had read about it, been told about it, but had never actually seen it. Jewish doctors did not get the residencies necessary to put into practice what they had learned in theory, but other doctors did. Instead, the Jewish doctors were sent out to remote clinics immediately after graduation.

Kamal left the consulting room, and the half dozen patients who sat around the waiting room stopped their chattering and stood up. He nodded, they nodded back, murmuring something which included the word *'Duktor'* used several times. He went through the arched passageway to the sitting room, took out a thick book from the trunk, placed it on the table, and began to leaf through it. Urinary tract infection – just as he thought. He closed the book and went back into the waiting room. Everyone stopped chattering and stood up, showing respect. Kamal nodded, they nodded back. Kamal went back into the consulting room, leaned over close to the mother and baby and said, 'The baby will be alright, don't be so worried. An injection of penicillin is all he needs.'

She looked confused, in an unstable state that could have as easily tipped into exalted happiness as into deep despair. Kamal smiled to reassure her. She looked to Abu-Rahman for explanation. Abu-Rahman was stunned; this was not how it was supposed to be.

'Tell *her* I'm going to give the baby an injection, and the baby will be okay.'

Abu-Rahman reluctantly did. The mother smiled and wrapped her baby back into his swaddling. Kamal left the consulting room, and everyone in the waiting room stood up. He nodded, they nodded back, but this time they smiled. They could hear what was going on in the consulting room. He went into the storeroom-cum-pharmacy and asked the male nurse, Samir, for a syringe.

'*Duktor*, I don't have any syringes. None are ready,' Samir said. 'We only use syringes in the afternoon.'

'Get one ready for me.'

'*Duktor!* It'll take time. I have to light up the primus, boil the water, and sterilize the syringe for half an hour.'

'Have we got any penicillin?' asked Kamal.

'No, *Duktor*. None in the stores.'

Kamal was incredulous. 'We have no penicillin?'

'We do have penicillin, in the private stock that *Duktor* Salman left behind.'

'We'll use that, 10 mils.'

Samir stood aghast, with his mouth open.

When the baby's mother emerged from the consulting room to wait for the syringe to be sterilized, she was greeted with smiles by the other patients. An animated chat weaved through the room, with exclamations and a mixture of bewilderment and fascination.

'Who is this new doctor?' someone enquired. 'He must be a communist,' another ventured, in a hushed tone.

Kamal picked up the syringe glass barrel with a pair of tongs from the sterilizing metal box, which a disgruntled male nurse had just handed to him. He placed it on a towel that he had spread on the table, used the tongs to pick up the plunger, and placed that next to the barrel. Then he did the same with the hypodermic needle.

When all the components were cold enough to handle, Kamal inserted the plunger into the open end of the barrel and clicked the needle into position at the other end, and set the plunger to the 10 millilitres on the barrel. He picked up the vial containing the liquid penicillin, wiped its rubber top with an alcohol swab, and pushed the needle forcibly through it. He then pushed the plunger in as far as it could go, forcing air into the vial. Turning it upside down, he extracted the penicillin into the syringe. He pulled the needle out from the vial and, with the needle pointing upwards, pushed the plunger gently to expel any air that might have entered the syringe. Small droplets of liquid emerged from the tiny hole at the end of the needle. He was now ready to insert the protruding, large metal object into the baby's little thigh. The mother carefully watched the doctor's every move. She had heard of these magical instruments which some called the 'devil's needle', but had never come across one.

Kamal gestured to the mother to remove the swaddling, which she did reluctantly, having just realized how frighteningly large the needle was. Kamal pinched the flesh of the baby's thigh tightly with the forefinger and thumb of his left hand, and held the needle ready to penetrate the baby's skin. The baby, who just happened to be having one of his rare moments of sleep, woke up and started whimpering. Kamal pushed the needle sharply into the flesh between his forefinger and thumb, and gently squeezed the liquid into the baby's thigh. The baby inhaled sharply, taking in an amount of air that seemed far in excess of what his small lungs could handle, and held his breath for what seemed to be an eternity, though, in reality, it was not more than one or two seconds. His face went red, orange, and then pale. Everyone, including the waiting patients, held their breath. Had the doctor killed him? The baby suddenly let go its breath and produced an ear-splitting scream that seemed to echo around the valley. This produced a burst of laughter and joy from everyone. The baby's mother held the baby tightly in her arms and cried.

As the mother began to leave, Kamal told her to come back tomorrow for another injection. Abu-Rahman reluctantly translated what he said, to the obvious delight of the mother.

'When the word goes round that you're giving free injections,' said Abu-Rahman, after the mother had left and the door was closed, 'no one will turn up to your private practice and where will that leave us?' He went on to explain: 'You see, *Duktor*, those with money go to Mosul, and those with no money come to the public clinic. Those who can afford a little come to the private clinic for a better service. Now, they have no incentive to do that.'

'How many people usually turn up to the clinic in the morning?' asked Kamal.

'Ten, fifteen, sometimes twenty, but never more than twenty-five.'

'Let's see if we can make that one hundred.'

After a pause, Kamal continued. 'If we get one hundred through the door, we'll have a party.'

It was later in the afternoon when Kamal was arranging some of the books that Abu-Rahman came in.

'Sorry to interrupt, *Duktor*, but a man outside insists on seeing you. He says his son is very ill and he wants you to pay a home visit. I said the fee is 3 dinars. He said he cannot afford that. I suggested that he brings his son to the clinic tomorrow morning, but he said his son may not last that long. Shall I get rid of him?'

Kamal placed the two books in his hands on the table and said, 'Get my bag.'

When Kamal entered the waiting room, a man in his forties, in traditional but shabby clothes, with a big turban, was pacing up and down. He stopped when he saw the doctor.

'*Duktor*,' he said, followed by words Kamal could not understand.

Kamal interrupted him. 'How much can you afford?'

Taken aback, the man hesitated, and then said, 'Quarter of a dinar.'

Kamal handed him the bag to carry. '*Imshi*, show me the way.' The man took the bag and walked out, followed by the doctor. Abu-Rahman shook his head in disbelief. 'At this rate, we'll have no private practice at all,' he murmured to himself.

Weeks went by, and the clinic became busier and busier. Kamal began to acquire a reputation as someone who cared for the patients. Many seeking his help spent hours travelling long distances on mountain tracks, walking or riding a mule to come to his clinic. The one-hundred patient threshold was reached and exceeded. A joyful party was had. The private practice was even more subscribed. The talk in the market place was: 'If the doctor treats free patients like this, how much better would he treat those who are prepared to pay?' They never had a doctor who treated them with such consideration and respect, and, above all, someone who spoke their language; for Kamal soon began to be able to understand the gist of a conversation with a patient. Within days of arriving, he had picked up several words in Kurdish, and in a short time he began to speak the language much like a native. He no longer had to depend on, what to him seemed, dubious translation by the caretaker. On occasions, he even wore their bright-coloured national costume, and he looked like a Kurdish prince, or so they told him. His popularity alerted the authorities, and the Chief of Police was asked to investigate if Kamal was organizing an anti-government political cell.

The summer turned into autumn, and the autumn into winter. Kamal woke up one morning and everything was white; everything was wrapped in a blanket of snow; bright, fresh snow, like soft cotton covering the roofs, the tracks, the mountains, and the trees. He had never seen snow before, and marvelled at the sight of snowflakes lazily swirling in the air, moving this way and that, before settling gently on the other snowflakes that had taken the same path.

He sat down and started a letter to Rosette, his second letter that week.

5

Six months later

ALTHOUGH HE WAS the eldest of her eight children, she knew that Kamal was the most vulnerable. It had been six months since he went to the mountainous region of Iraq where people spoke a different language, isolated, with the nearest town over 100 miles away. Um-Kamal knew, from the numerous letters he wrote home, that her eldest son needed her.

'Kamal needs me,' she told her husband, 'and that's why I have to go.' Abu-Kamal was happy for his wife to take that responsibility; he couldn't, as he lacked the courage, and skills, that his wife seemed to have in abundance.

So, it was one evening in late May when Um-Kamal arrived at the Baghdad Central Railway Station to take the overnight train to Mosul; the one daily train to Mosul that leaves Baghdad at 5 o'clock in the evening and arrives in Mosul early the next day, over a distance of some 250 miles. Women not accompanied by an adult male always took a young son or daughter on such journeys, as a form of protection and a show of respectability. Um-Kamal took her youngest son, five-year-old Farouk, with her.

The station was packed with people pulling and pushing luggage of all shapes and sizes, some carrying sacks on their heads, walking up and down the platform looking for a seat. The train arrived at the platform some two hours before the time of departure and was immediately swamped with people, mainly young men, the majority of whom did not want to travel, but to occupy a space to be sold to a traveller for a fee. Very soon, every space on the wood and metal benches was occupied.

On the platform, there were hawkers and peddlers outshouting each other in their efforts to get the attention of travellers for their merchandise, from tea and cakes, to sunflower and pumpkin seeds, as well as slippers, shoes, and assorted headwear. The mass of people were concentrated in the rear nine carriages of the train. Only one or two passengers, with porters carrying heavy leather suitcases, could be seen in the front four. It was as if there was an invisible line that no one dared to cross. The first four carriages were second class, with sleeping compartments hanging above the upholstered benches. The luxurious first class had an oak interior, electric fans and cushioned, red leather benches which the attendant would turn into comfortable beds with linen sheets and fluffy blankets. Um-Kamal and her son were travelling third class.

Um-Kamal was not interested in the hawkers, or anyone offering her a seat on the train. She threw her ageing case secured by two hefty brown leather straps onto the landing of the first carriage that seemed to be less crowded than the others. She put her right foot on the recessed high step, with her right hand gripping the handle bar, and holding Farouk's left wrist tightly behind her with her left hand. With one forceful movement, she heaved herself and her son onto the train. She looked into the carriage; all benches were fully occupied, in some cases with more people than the benches could reasonably be expected to accommodate. Um-Kamal walked along the middle aisle, pushing her heavy case in front of her. With Farouk in tow, she tried to find the slightest chink in the mass of humanity before her that she could exploit. She stopped next to the bench that had one passenger fewer than the other benches. With a smile, and an obvious hint that she was a woman with a child, she gestured to the four young men to move a little and make some space, which they did, with a slight air of embarrassment. She perched herself at the end of the bench, and Farouk sat on her lap. One of the young men then helped make space for her heavy case on the luggage rack above them.

At 5PM precisely, the guard blew his whistle – one short burst followed by a much longer one, ending with a short burst identical to the first. Hawkers, who were offering their wares to the passengers inside the carriages, started to leave, without much hint of a hurry. The steam engine, the giant Robert Stephenson & Hawthorns PC class 4-6-2, roared and puffed, commanding the resting wagons' attention, in the manner of a sergeant major on a parade ground. The wagons bumped forwards and backwards into each other, clinking and clunking, and when the couplings were taut and their screeching ended, they started to move, reluctantly at first, then gathering speed with every puff the monster engine belched out into the clean, clear air of early evening Baghdad. The train left the station packed with a cargo of perspiring human souls and luggage of all kinds: wooden boxes and metal-armoured cases, sacks and bags and Ali Baba jugs, a cockerel and a goat – all trundled along the seemingly endless track, taking in cities large and small.

The monster engine settled to a steady puffing rate with the train moving at a steady speed. The passengers began to settle for the long journey ahead, occupying all possible spaces. One man lifted his wicker bird cage onto his lap, so that two pleasant young students could sit, having earlier given their seats to a pregnant woman and her shy young daughter. Another man, with a large white beard, a stick, and heavy concave glasses that seemed to do little to improve his eyesight, sat next to the goat which he regularly disciplined, using his stick every time the goat had it in its mind to stretch its hind legs. Then someone started to sing a ballad, but soon gave up, as others failed to join in. A baby cried somewhere down the carriage, and an offer came from a short but sturdy man, with a pronounced, thin nose and fluffy hair, to milk the goat to give the baby a drink. However, the offer was politely declined and, instead, a green and yellow striped candy stick, in the shape of a dummy, was pushed into the baby's mouth which immediately stopped its crying. A cockerel, having tried several roosting spots, including the very inviting flat turban of a startled man in a Lawrence of Arabia robe (that was more suitable for a journey on a horse than in a train), decided to settle in Farouk's lap. He gently stroked its bright red and black feathers, but it pecked his fingers playfully. Nevertheless, he was happy.

Before the train could reach its renowned maximum speed of 65 miles per hour, it began to decelerate, in anticipation of the next stop, and eventually came to rest with a huge sigh of relief from the monster engine. The wagons squeaked and screeched, and bumped into each other, before resting at ease. Everyone looked out, shaking their heads, gesticulating with their arms, and muttering all possible permutations of 'no', 'full', 'no place', and 'somewhere else'. Anxious faces appeared and disappeared at the small glass window which was a quarter of the way down the exit door, except for one face, the last face, which refused to go away. Distorted by the irregular glass, it stared back at the occupants. The engine puffed and commanded attention, and the wagons began to bump into each other again as the couplings became taut. The train started to move, gathering speed, but the face stayed glued to the small glass on the exit door, looking at the faces looking back at it, as the train gradually reached the critical speed which would cripple anyone foolhardy enough to entertain any idea of stepping off onto the hard, barren ground. It was at this moment that those nearest the exit door turned the heavy handle and unlocked it. The face now materialized, with a body attached, carrying a small grey sack covered with soot dust. He was helped inside and instantly people started to shuffle this way and that, with jugs and jars being placed on top of each other. The goat, being squeezed into an ever-smaller space, expressed its displeasure by spitting into the face of a man busy eating a watermelon. The newly arrived passenger stumbled into the freshly cleared space on the floor, and was soon engaged in conversation, and offered water and sweets; he was now one of them. At the next station, the same ritual was enacted – faces peering through the exit door window, looking at heads shaking, arms gesticulating, and mouths muttering.

Halfway through the journey, when most passengers were asleep or trying to sleep, there was a murmur among the passengers. Um-Kamal and her son opened their eyes and looked out. They saw what seemed like a slowly moving reflection of their train; an identical train, with identical carriages, loaded with identical human and animal cargo, moving in the opposite direction, within touching distance.

'It is the Baghdad-bound train,' Um-Kamal whispered in her son's ear. The two trains slowly, imperceptibly, came to a halt in a badly lit station. The station master was waving a white and black flag. Another man had a whistle in his mouth, ready to blow. Sleepy eyes met sleepy eyes, tired faces looked at tired faces; greetings were exchanged and some attempt was made at conversation. Someone asked about the weather in Mosul. 'When did you leave Mosul?' another asked, randomly.

After a while, the train started to move. Farouk felt disorientated, as his eyes perceived movement, but his body did not feel the sensation of a moving train.

'The other train is moving off,' Um-Kamal said. He looked up and he could see the platform's cast iron lamp post with a dim lantern hanging from the top. It remained stationary, and his disorientation disappeared.

At the break of dawn, the train came to an unexpected halt in the middle of nowhere. Veterans of the Baghdad-to-Mosul journey were quick to inform those whose journey was their first that the train was about to enter a tunnel. There was much speculation on the length of the tunnel, from half a mile to three-and-a-half miles; similarly, with the time it would take the train to reach the other end. The two college students mused that if the time it takes the train to reach the end of the tunnel is known, and its speed when it leaves the tunnel can be guessed at, then the length of the tunnel could be calculated. Someone produced a stop watch from his pocket. Looking out of the window, Farouk observed the train driver stepping out of his cab, and he was quickly engaged in conversation with someone whom he assumed to be the tunnel keeper. 'What could they be talking about?' he wondered. After exchanging a few words, the engine started puffing again. The man with the stop watch pressed the start button harder than necessary. The engine puffed and huffed, and the train gathered speed. Cooling water jugs that were hanging out were brought in, windows were closed, and pulled shut as far as was possible. Soon, fumes sneaked through the numerous cracks in the fabric of the train, filling the carriage with black steam and soot. Someone coughed, another joined in, and soon most of the passengers were coughing. The train seemed to go faster than before, an illusion caused by the proximity of the train to the tunnel walls. Suddenly, the stars were visible again as the train cleared the tunnel, to a chorus of relief and joy.

'It took three minutes and twenty-one seconds,' someone said. 'Faster than normal.'

The speed of the train as it left the tunnel caused some controversy, generating heated debate; there was no consensus. Farouk was intrigued. 'Can you really find the length of the tunnel that way?'

'Go to sleep,' said his mother.

The train started its deceleration long before it finally came to a halt at Mosul Central, at seven in the morning. Leaving the train proved to be as chaotic as boarding it; it was not for the faint hearted. Everyone seemed to be in a great hurry to get out. Luggage was retrieved from under other luggage; cases grabbed from overhead shelves, where they had sat squeezed in among other luggage throughout the journey. Some pulled boxes and baskets out over the heads of other passengers, but most hurled their belongings out through the windows to waiting friends or relatives who came to meet the train. There was shoving and pushing, greetings and shouting, and much cursing – and as many apologies for doing the cursing. Two young men helped Um-Kamal push her heavy case through the window and dropped it onto the rough platform. Um-Kamal was reminded of the last time she was at the station – a young child of ten with striking blue eyes, unusual in that part of the world, and elegant with good looks. Born in the Kurdish city of Kirkuk, among a thriving Jewish community that went back thousands of years, she was caught up in the great movement of people that accompanied the First World War. With her father conscripted into the Ottoman army, from whence nobody was expected to return, and with the British army in control of the north, her mother decided to move the family to Baghdad. It is a story she often told her children; of how British squaddies heavily dressed and perspiring in their rough khaki uniforms and hard helmets, with rifles slung on their shoulders, pushed them into a rickety train, shouting at them in a language she could not understand. One word stuck in her mind: '*fackin*' – a word she forever associated with the British army. It was much later that she became aware of the actual word she had been repeating to her young children all those many years: 'fucking'.

They spent the night with the Nemruds, a Christian family that Um-Kamal knew from the days when her family lived in that part of the country. They slept on wicker mattresses on the roof, as is the custom in Iraq, where summer temperatures can reach 50 degrees in the day and 30 degrees at night. The roof becomes a communal bedroom, and love making becomes a quiet affair carried out under the stars, in silence. The neighbouring house had had a bereavement, and the mourning ritual was in full swing in the open courtyard. The relatives of the deceased hired professional mourners to provide the requisite level of wailing and crying that befits the soul of the departed. The wailers took their task seriously, and kept up their lamentations, weeping, whining and crying all night. It wasn't till day break that their job was done. No sooner had they left, than a cockerel decided it was time to take over and began to crow loudly and persistently.

'Someone throttle that bird,' Farouk heard his mother say, under her breath.

Without much sleep, but with a good breakfast of *khubz*, the oval-shaped Iraqi flat bread, apricot jam and delicious *geymer*, the traditional rich, thick cream, Um-Kamal and her son departed to the central square, where the cries of street vendors mingled with those offering transport to every destination within a 100-mile radius – from Erbil and Kirkuk, to the south, to Duhok and Zakho, to the north. One destination was Aqrah. Um-Kamal approached a driver standing next to a black-blue Oldsmobile with elaborate head lights, and even more elaborate tail lights, who was shouting 'Aqrah, 2 dinars... Aqrah, 2 dinars.' A haggle ensued, as is customary in these circumstances, with Um-Kamal insisting that her son go for free.

'Two dinars, and the boy goes for free,' was her opening bid.

'Do me a favour; the boy will occupy a seat.'

'He is only three.'

Farouk hunched his back, trying to look small.

'Three! More like six.'

'He can sit on my lap.'

'He's a big boy. I'll lose a passenger.'

'Half a dinar for the boy.'

'A dinar.'

'A dinar, and he gets a seat.'

He started loading Um-Kamal's ageing case into the spacious boot of the American car.

'A dinar, and he sits on your lap.'

Um-Kamal opened her purse and gave the driver 2½ dinars in notes.

The driver stretched out his hand. 'Half a dinar more.'

She handed him 200 fils in change. 'Here, a quarter of a dinar.'

Counting the change. 'That's still 50 fils short.'

She gave the man 50 fils, and asked, 'When will you be leaving?'

'Not till I get five or six more passengers,' he said, and continued calling, 'Aqrah, Aqrah... 2 dinars only.'

The tarmac road was narrow, only a car wide; it dissected the empty plains of Mosul, and stretched far into the distance, where a mirage of blue flowing water kept making an appearance from time to time. Um-Kamal pulled her abaya around her, sat at the back, next to the door behind the driver, and tucked Farouk in next to her, providing a barrier between her and the other passengers, all male. The driver kept one hand loosely on the steering wheel, lifting it when making a gesture or lighting a cigarette, which he did often, while the other hand was dangling out of the window, except when he was holding a cigarette, which he often did, in which case he rested his left elbow on the window ledge, keeping the cigarette away from the wind. The voice of Saleh Al-Kuwaity, the renowned Jewish master of Iraqi folk music, rolled out from the short-wave car radio. The road was empty, except for the few cars travelling in the opposite direction; and when they met, they pulled over to the right to avoid a collision, leaving a cloud of dust behind them.

An hour into the journey and the terrain began to change from a barren uninhabited landscape to the lush grassland of the alluvial steppe plains; the imposing dark silhouette of Jabil Sinjar, the Sinjar mountain range, could be seen in the background. The Oldsmobile began to groan as the car started the long climb up the Sinjar. The driver forced the column gear stick into third, and then into second, and pressed on up the winding, steep road.

'Abu el-Quwad!', he swore, and immediately apologized to Um-Kamal. Just when the engine was about to give up, the summit was reached. Following a short hiatus, an even-steeper downhill zig-zagging road became visible. The driver turned off the engine, allowing the car to free-wheel down to the valley, taking sharp corners at alarmingly high speeds. Um-Kamal held onto her son tightly and closed her eyes. The alarm of the other passengers was evident from the sudden end of the random conversation that had so far alternated with the grumble of the

vexed engine. They swung this way and that with each hair-pin turn. The driver made no allowances for the new driving conditions, still smoking a cigarette in one hand, and manoeuvring the wheel with the other. There was no visible urgency in his movements, as the car screeched, making 180-degree turns every few hundred yards, all the way down to the valley below. The scenery was breath-taking; rocky mountains punctuated with lush trees, goats hanging onto the mountain face, a fast-flowing stream at the bottom. Red-beaked Chukar partridges scattered as the car sped by. Eurasian buzzards and Steppe eagles circled above, but it was not a time to appreciate the sheer beauty of the raw, brutal nature. A muffled sigh of relief could be heard as the automobile reached the bottom of the valley, and the driver put the engine back into gear. They crossed the fast-flowing stream, scattering a herd of goats. The herdsman, sitting in the shade of a tree, looked on with complete lack of interest. Farouk wished the car would stop for him to step into the fresh crystal-clear cold water of the stream. The driver put the engine into second gear and began another climb.

It was a relief when the car finally came to a halt at Aqrah market square. No sooner had Um-Kamal stepped out with her son in tow, than Aziz, the porter, grabbed her heavy trunk from the boot of the car and, with the help of the driver, put it on his back and started walking up towards the path leading to the clinic.

'*Um el-Duktor, ahlan*, welcome, *ahlan*,' said the café owner, who was the first to greet her. 'Did you have a good journey?'

'Yes – a bit hairy; but yes.'

'Ah, Abu-Muslim does tend to drive fast, but he gets you here quickly.'

A sweet stall vendor was cracking sunflower seeds with his right hand, then feeding them into his mouth in a continuous stream of yellow beads – expertly removing the shells and spitting them onto the floor. 'And what is your name?' he asked Um-Kamal's son.

'Farouk.'

'And how old are you?'

'He's five,' replied Um-Kamal, on Farouk's behalf. '*El-Duktor*'s youngest brother.'

'So, Farouk, would you like a sweet?' asked the stall vendor, pointing to a jar of brightly coloured sweets that seemed to have more flies hovering around its half open top than items within it. Two brothers of similar age, who were observing the proceedings, looked at Farouk with undisguised envy.

'*La, shukran*; no, thanks,' replied Farouk, in a low, not-wishing-to-offend voice.

'Ah! He is a shy boy,' responded the stall vendor, and, removing the top of the sweet jar, he scattered the hovering flies, and pulled out a slightly wilting, bright-yellow, flat lollipop in the shape of a smiling sun. Sensing danger, the flies escaped in a rush, the more persistent ones remaining glued to the sticky sweets, including one or two still stuck to the smiling sun. Um-Kamal intercepted the stall vendor on his way to give the lollipop to her son, and holding it between her fingers said, 'My little boy doesn't like sweets.'

'A five-year-old who doesn't like sweets?' mused the stall vendor.

Um-Kamal handed the smiling sun, with a fly on top, to the two brothers. The older one grabbed it and ran. The younger one gave chase and, in the process, stepped on the tail of the stray market dog, who up to this point had been deliriously asleep under one of the café's wicker chairs. The dog howled, as wild animals do when in sudden pain, barked, looked around, and ran after the two boys.

The stall vendor, shaking his head, replaced the top on the sweet jar. Most of the flies went back into the jar, while others kept up a noisy hover around its half-open top.

Um-Kamal looked at her trunk disappearing halfway up the mountain path.

'*El-Duktor*'s house is this way, just follow Aziz,' said the café owner.

Abu-Rahman and his wife were waiting at the door when Um-Kamal arrived. The steps that connected one street level to the next took their toll, and she was out of breath when she finally got to the clinic where her son worked.

'*Ahlan, ahlan*, welcome,' said Abu-Rahman. 'You must be tired.'

'You must be tired,' repeated his wife. 'Come in, come in. I'll make you some chai.'

Abu-Rahman, addressing Farouk, said, 'And you, beautiful young boy, you must be Fakri.'

Farouk didn't like the way Abu-Rahman looked at him. 'No! It is Farouk.'

'Of course, Farouk,' said Abu-Rahman, pinching the young boy's cheek, in a manner that Farouk thought was inappropriate.

'Where is Kamal?' asked Um-Kamal.

'*El-Duktor?* He is out on a call,' said Abu-Rahman.

'He knows you are here,' said his wife. 'News travels fast in this small village. Everyone knows *el-Duktor*'s mother and his young brother are here.'

When Kamal finally came back, Um-Kamal held him in her arms, feeling all parts of his body, as if she was inspecting a watermelon for bruises.

'Sorry, I had to see...'

'*B'dalak*, you lost so much weight,' she said, with the extreme exaggeration that is the tradition in such circumstances. 'You're all skin and bones. There is nothing left of you.'

'I'm fine,' said Kamal, 'and you brought Farouk with you.' To Farouk's delight, Kamal roughly ruffled his hair. Though Kamal was smiling broadly and was obviously happy to see them both, Um-Kamal could sense that he was not at ease with himself.

That night, when Farouk was fast asleep, Kamal spoke of his feelings of isolation from the family and his loneliness. He admitted feeling guilty about Sasson.

'I should have protected him,' he said. 'He was just a child, a teenager.'

'You couldn't do anything. It's not your fault,' Um-Kamal assured him.

'I know it's not my fault, that I'm not responsible, but I have the feeling that I am.'

'Don't distress yourself.'

'How is he? Has he been tortured?'

'He's fine, doing well. Soon he will be out.'

'Did he explain what happened? Why he confessed? Did he say anything?'

'He doesn't talk about it.'

Later, Um-Kamal could hear her son muttering in his sleep. She couldn't make out what he was saying.

6

2003 – Um-Kamal, Ramat Gan

'You seem so certain. Did he tell you what happened?' Farouk asked his mother, as he sat in an armchair in her lounge, in her sparse apartment in Ramat Gan, sipping tea from a delicate, thin glass cup, with a gold strip around its rim.

They had just been to the cemetery to visit Abu-Kamal's grave. At the graveside, in a drab cemetery on the outskirts of Ramat Gan, Um-Kamal spoke loudly as she swept the dry soil off the grave, picked up a stone from the ground and placed it on the flat top of the grave as is the Jewish custom.

'Abu-Kamal, Farouk is here, your youngest son has come to see you.' A chill went down Farouk's spine, a shiver went up his neck, which made his hair stand on end. Um-Kamal was talking to his father as if he was there, as if he could hear. She actually believed her husband, dead for five years, could hear her, that she could communicate with him. What a relief that must be for her, thought Farouk.

'Everyone expected Kamal to go down, what with him being older,' Um-Kamal told her son. 'But no! Kamal goes free and Sasson gets eight years. Eight years! That is a very long time for anyone, especially a sixteen-year-old.'

'What are you saying?' asked Farouk.

'No one ever got out free,' said Um-Kamal, turning to Farouk. 'Everyone got five, seven, ten, or even more years. Only those who turned informants, betrayed the Party, got off.'

'You are not suggesting that Kamal betrayed the Party?' asked Farouk.

'No, of course not,' said Um-Kamal. 'But it is a mystery to me.'

'What does Sasson say?'

'He doesn't speak about it,' said Um-Kamal. 'No one does.'

'But Kamal never saw Sasson; they were kept in separate cells.'

'Same cell, different cells! Eh...'

With a deep sigh, she continued, 'You know, the tragedy is, had Sasson waited for four or five hours, till the morning at least, both of them would have been out.'

The windows of the apartment were wide open. It was hot, and there was no air conditioning. An exhausted great thrush, whose 20 centimetre height belied its 'great' label, perched its dainty yellow feet on the window ledge.

'Give it a piece of bread,' said Um-Kamal, pointing to the bread bin over the fridge freezer. 'It comes to the window every day for some food.'

Farouk tore off a piece of pita and presented it to the bird, which had its yellow beak wide open. It extended its small neck as far as it could without tipping over the edge, and closed its beak, snapping the bread and scratching Farouk's fingers in the process. Farouk instinctively pulled his hand back and the sudden movement frightened the bird, which flapped its wings and flew away with the whole piece of bread in its beak. Farouk watched as the pita began to disintegrate, leaving the bird with a tiny crumb.

'Did you ever join?' asked Farouk.

'The Party?'

'The Communist Party.'

'They asked me many times, but I wouldn't.'

'But you did work for them,' said Farouk. 'You took risks.'

'Yes, I did a lot for them; more than most. I did it for Sasson, like any mother would. That's what mothers do.'

'You must have had communist sympathies, surely.'

'*Ibni*, anyone who wanted to change the country for the better had... how did you put it…? Sympathies, communist sympathies. But joining the Party, no!'

'Why not?'

'It wasn't my thing. Anyway, after Fahd was hanged, it all went wrong. He was a lovely man.'

'Did you know Fahd? Did you meet him?'

'I didn't know who he was; no one knew who he really was. I didn't know it at the time, but yes, I did meet him.'

'That is fascinating. How did you meet him?' asked Farouk.

'It was at my uncle's, Abu-Sabra's, house. I went there for something or other, I can't remember, and he was in the lounge. His real name was Yusuf. I thought he was Jewish. He said: "Um-Kamal, it's a pleasure to meet you." He had a soft, quiet voice, and a very pleasant, intelligent face, with thick eyebrows and a black, tidy moustache.'

'I remember people talking about him in hushed tones,' said Farouk. 'He was greatly admired.'

'They adored him. The Party adored him. I tell you what, had he lived long enough, they would have disowned him and called him a traitor.'

'A traitor?'

'Look what happened to Stalin. One day Stalin was a saint, he could do no wrong. The next day he became a monster. What's his name... Karoshov...'

'Khrushchev.'

'Yes, Karoshov.'

'Khrushchev, Nikita Khrushchev.'

'Yes, Kharoshev. He took over, and said Stalin was a bastard, and everyone said yes, Stalin is a bastard.'

She put her tea cup down onto its transparent glass saucer. 'Anyway,' she said, 'why are you so interested in digging up the past? You come here for a week, and all you do is ask questions.'

'I want to know what happened. It's my past, my background. I was five, maybe six, when all of this was going on. I was too young to understand. I don't remember much – only snippets, reflections that may or may not be true.'

'You're going to America, to Canada, talking to everyone, raking up the past. How do you know that anyone wants to go over the past? If you keep digging, you may find something you regret, things you do not want to know.'

'Or things I need to know,' said Farouk quietly.

'Seeking the truth is natural. It's seductive, but not necessarily fruitful.'

'The truth never hurts.'

'The truth always hurts,' said Um-Kamal.

7

1951 – Qamber Ali, Baghdad

IF YOU OPENED the window at Um-Kamal's house, you could hear Radio Moscow loud and clear; the whole street could hear it. To be caught listening to Radio Moscow would land anyone in jail; but not Abu-Jasim. He was the neighbourhood spy. Just as every neighbourhood has a baker and a butcher, it also has a government informer, most of whom carry out their work in secret, listening to people talking, observing people's behaviour and habits, where they go, who they see, and with whom they are friendly. Not Abu-Jasim. He had the novel idea of acting like an anti-government agitator in order to attract anti-government agitators; posing as a communist to attract communists. He didn't seem to have a job, or to be in need of one. He would walk around the place, engage people in conversation and openly and loudly slag off the government and the King.

It is the same tactic employed by barbers, most of whom are in the pay of the government. They engage their customers, who are trapped in the barber's chair, in a conversation about the price of bread, the shortage of eggs, the plight of the country, or the duplicity of the British in the politics of the Middle East, all in the hope that the customers will reciprocate and reveal their political tendencies, so they can report them to the secret police, *al-Mukhabarat*. It was an unwritten, but religiously and universally observed, rule never to say anything to a barber, other than superficial chatter and, where necessary, express love for the King and support for the government of the day. But Abu-Jasim took these strategies to extremes. Needless to say, the only 'communist' he ever caught was the neighbourhood idiot, who suffered from some form of psychosis and who talked in a loud voice to his demons, and who, on one occasion, had the misfortune of joining the local spy in shouting anti-government slogans in the market place. Local people quickly bundled him away and calmed him down. He was arrested the very next day, and was never seen again.

But the windows were shut and Ezra tuned the short-wave radio to the BBC World Service, listening to the six o'clock news. As usual, it was dominated by the Korean War. Ezra kept a map of Korea on the wall, with coloured drawing pins showing the positions of the two armies. On this occasion, there was a report from the front, with a correspondent reporting live on an assault by the American army on a village somewhere in that unfortunate country. In the background, bursts of machine gun fire could be heard.

Um-Kamal, listening to the commotion, asked Ezra why were the Americans fighting in Korea? To the sound of continuous gun fire, Ezra explained. 'You see, Nana, for every bullet fired, Uncle Sam gets five pence in his pocket. That's why they are fighting a war over there.'

It was the eve of Passover, and preparation for the next day's feast were under way. But Um-Kamal had to leave it aside, because she had to serve tonight's dinner. Dinner was a big affair. The siblings were neatly divided into two groups: the older four – Rosette, the eldest, and three sons, Kamal, Ezra and Sasson, born eighteen months apart; and a second group – Elias, Layla, Sa'id and Farouk, also born eighteen months apart. In the period between the two groups of four older and four younger siblings, Um-Kamal and Abu-Kamal were not inactive in terms of procreation. They had one daughter who was stillborn, whom they called Kamila, and before that a boy, Benjamin, who died from meningitis at the tender age of eight months – a baby of astounding beauty with large blue eyes and a fair complexion, regarded by all as the most beautiful baby boy they had ever seen. His death was brought about by a curse, *al-hassad*, or envy. He died the day after a passing stranger looked at him and said, 'What a beautiful baby!' Superstition has it that it was the curse of that woman's *hassad* which brought about the death of the young baby. When her youngest boy, Farouk, was born with fair complexion and blonde hair, comparisons were made with Benjamin; from that moment, and until Farouk was three, Um-Kamal took the precaution of hiding his face whenever she took him out. He was considered to be vulnerable to *al-hassad* of strangers that might lead to the same fate that befell Benjamin.

Every time she prepared dinner, Um-Kamal was reminded of her son in prison, for she had to set one place fewer at the dinner table. The sadness she felt had not subsided with the passage of time; a sadness that, in some respects, was deeper than the one she felt for her dead son Benjamin. It's now more than two years since Sasson was taken away. His imprisonment caused more pain because, unlike Benjamin, there had been no closure. But she never allowed her sadness and pain to show, or at least she didn't think anyone noticed. She had to stay strong, stronger than most, if only to compensate for her husband's inability to cope with the mishaps of life. She had a responsibility to keep the family safe, alive, and well – an onerous task that always fell on the shoulders of women; the much-maligned housewives.

True, she had her eldest daughter, Rosette, to help. Rosette was a tower of strength, the first port of call for all of her brothers and her sister for guidance, advice, and help, as well as emotional support.

Rosette had looked after the younger ones since they were born, helped with the household chores as was expected of girls and, at the same time, went to school at an early age, unlike the custom in those times and that place. She worked hard and managed to get high grades in her baccalaureate exams to go to university to study medicine. For a girl, a Jewish girl, to do that, from the rough side of town, was unheard of.

With good looks, intelligence and education, and prospects as a doctor, the most respected of all professions, she could get any husband she desired. There would be no need for a dowry, Um-Kamal confided in Abu-Kamal. She could marry a wealthy, prosperous man; something her parents hoped would help to alleviate their almost hopeless task of keeping the large family fed and clothed. But, as fate would have it, she fell in love with Murad, a Jew with Clark Gable looks, including the thin moustache, who was in the same year of medical school as her, but with even less money. It was his elder brother's financial support that put him through university – something that Murad never failed to mention, at every opportunity, as an example of selfless generosity. A young man with obvious intelligence and intellectual capacity, he was scarred by a chronic lack of self-confidence and the need to impress, occasioned by the sudden bankruptcy of his father's business, which rendered the family almost destitute when he was seven. He was fond of casually dropping the English word 'darling' into conversation. 'Darling, it's the best,' was a catchphrase of his, referring to anything that he owned or was closely associated with.

To demonstrate his superiority, he found it necessary to denigrate others, to put them down, to make himself look a cut above.

The financial circumstances of his early years morphed into an unedifying respect for money, and people with money. He developed an insatiable desire to make money, coupled with a unique, bipolar combination of munificence on one hand and stinginess on the other; unpredictably switching from unbounded generosity to outright meanness almost at random. On one occasion, when courting Rosette, he had browbeaten a twelve-year-old who was selling toothbrushes in the street to make a few fils into handing him the rest of his stock of twenty brushes, for what must have been far less than the poor child had paid for them. Farouk, who accompanied the couple to give respectability to the courting, witnessed the haggling, and could see how difficult it was for the young trader to make the quick calculations necessary to ensure he was not left out of pocket. Murad, in his final year at medical school, bombarded him with one offer after another, each accompanied by an explanation of how generous it was. Farouk could see that his older sister was embarrassed, but she always took the side of Murad in such situations. Murad was pleased with his display of haggling prowess, and the toothbrushes turned out to be for his pet dog, which he called Bony, and which he acquired in order to emulate the wealthier part of the Jewish community. The baffled and frightened face of the young trader stayed with Farouk for the rest of his life.

Um-Kamal's and her husband's attempts to dissuade their daughter from marrying Murad fell on deaf ears. She was deeply in love with him, and he was with her – of that there was no doubt. However, 'marriage is not just for love', and they urged her to think of her future security and financial stability. It was all to no avail, and her parents' dreams of a rich son-in-law to lift them out of poverty evaporated. Soon after, their hopes that once she began to earn money she would help out with the family finances were also dashed. Murad's obsession with money meant that he regarded Rosette's earnings, even before they got married, as his. So when Rosette graduated and started to work and she brought home her first monthly pay, it was Murad who came over and insisted that she hand it all over to him, to the dismay of Um-Kamal, her husband, and a perplexed Sa'id, who had witnessed that unedifying display of self-centred male dominance.

The family never went hungry. Um-Kamal and Abu-Kamal made sure of that. Um-Kamal may have gone to bed with an empty stomach, but none of her children did. Clothes and shoes were handed down from one brother to the next, and Layla's dresses and blouses were adapted from her older sister's discarded ones. Whenever something new was purchased, a celebratory atmosphere gripped the household, providing much-needed relief from the normal routine. The children did not feel any sort of envy towards those who had more money than them, and that was more or less everyone else. They all followed Abu-Kamal's strong belief that having brains was far superior to having money.

Abu-Kamal had a good job on the railways soon after he came to Baghdad with the British army that had fought its way up the Tigris from Basra. When the British army from India had landed at Basra, they had no one who spoke Arabic. There was an urgent need for interpreters. In Basra, there were very few people who could read and write Arabic, let alone speak English. Young Abu-Kamal – Menashi as he would have been known then to family and friends – was an exception, so he was quickly recruited to interpret for the commanding officers, among whom was General Frederick Stanley Maude, who captured Baghdad in 1917. Abu-Kamal was among the troops that broke the siege of Kut, where the shortage of food was such that a rat's tail could be sold for a few dinars (as he was fond of telling his children). Abu-Kamal was a captain in the British army when he entered Baghdad, driving a motorized bike, along with the mechanized division. It was during his time with the British that Abu-Kamal developed a deep fondness for anything that was English, so much so that he named his second son Ezra Maude, after the general – something that landed Ezra in trouble later. In particular, he admired the subtlety and sense of entitlement of the officer class, which was something he passed on to his children, who grew up thinking everything English was good, though not the British Empire. Abu-Kamal would have stayed in the British army except for Um-Kamal's father's refusal to have his daughter married to a man who would take her 'to the other side of the world'.

So, he managed to get a job in the railways, but Jews were later forbidden from working for the government, when the railways became a public utility. Therefore, Abu-Kamal had to retire with a small pension that wasn't sufficient to feed his large family. After a short spell of unemployment, he managed to find work as a clerk in a Jewish-run firm. The firm was formally owned by a Muslim, since Jews were at that time also forbidden from owning a business, but it was actually run by a Jewish friend of the family. Providing for eight children was hard at the best of times, but the restrictions on Jews doing certain jobs made it even harder. However, he managed to provide for the family regardless. As soon as they could, both Kamal and Ezra helped by working during school holidays, weekends and evenings, and they gave all they earned to their mother. There was no question in either Abu-Kamal's or his wife's mind that any of their sons could leave their education and get a job, as most other children did. Education was a top priority for Abu-Kamal, even if they had to go hungry.

'Food! Food is ready,' called Rosette who was helping her mother to prepare meat and okra stew. This was a favourite of Abu-Kamal, who was born in Amarah, where *bamia* – gravy of lamb with okra on a bed of white rice – was the traditional dish. This was the signal for everyone to race down the stairs. Farouk jumped on Kamal's shoulders, as he usually did. As they came down, they asked, in what had become a tradition since their father lost his job, and food had become scarce: '*A'am aw khas?*' 'General or individual?' If it was '*khas*', then the bread would be divided into equally sized slices, one for each of the children. If it was '*A'am*', then the bread would be in the middle of the table and family members helped themselves. The answer invariably was '*khas*'. Abu-Kamal and Um-Kamal ate later.

Everyone was looking forward to the Passover celebration the next day, especially the younger children, because the table would be full of food that the family could not normally afford to eat. In particular, Sa'id and Farouk looked forward to eating a whole boiled egg each, a luxury that they only experienced at that time of the year. But, before all that, there was the question of reading page after page of an undecipherable book written in Hebrew. The gist was obvious, but its precise meaning was not. Sa'id, the most studious of the younger children, and the most willing, was normally given the task of reading, which he did very competently. To relieve the boredom, which engulfed, to some degree or another, everyone, Ezra kept up a constant stream of humorous observations on the absurdity of the ritual, and the farcical nature of eating the food in a particular order. After certain verses had been read, everyone bowed their heads at specific times to convey observance of and subservience to what was being read out. Some of his utterances would certainly be considered heretical and seditious if heard by a more observant Jew. He regularly interjected with a subtle political comment; and when, to the obvious relief of everyone, they arrived at the last part, which was the bit that everyone understood and joined in with, more in relief than conviction: 'Next year we'll be in Jerusalem' – the sentiment that Jews have been required to reiterate at every Passover for 2,700 years – Ezra, to the evident enjoyment of his siblings, and the muted amusement of Abu-Kamal, substituted it with: 'Next year we'll have a revolution.'

'You'll get all of us in prison,' commented Um-Kamal, from her place away from the celebratory activities.

Um-Kamal did not join in the fun and excitement that were a feature of such celebrations in the household. There was little in terms of religious observance, other than the minimum, and even that was conducted with laughter. She sat separately, away from the rest of the family, as she had done on such occasions since Sasson was taken away from her. She had no favourites, although, as is the culture of that part of the world, boys were favoured more than girls, and Layla insisted that she was always given less food and affection than her contemporary brothers. Um-Kamal did feel deeply for Sasson.

The only other time the family had enough meat was when Abu-Kamal brought a ram home – something that some families did from time to time, as a cheaper source of food, usually to share with relatives and neighbours. The live ram with light-yellow fleece and two small protruding horns, which the children found intriguing, was unceremoniously bundled up the two sets of stairs to the roof, where it was kept to be 'fattened' before slaughter. Being taken away from its natural surroundings and offered left-over lettuce and cabbage leaves for food did not provide the perfect diet for a grass-eating animal. The ram lost weight, to the dismay of Abu-Kamal, and much recrimination from Um-Kamal. For Sa'id and Farouk, it was a piece of the countryside brought into the brick and mortar of inner-city Baghdad, and it provided endless enjoyment and fun, not just feeding the beast, but playing with it. They discovered that by pushing hard against its flat head, it would push back harder, and a contest quickly evolved to see who could push the ram furthest. The ram, in desperation or anger, would lunge at them from time to time, which provided even more amusement as the boys tried to avoid its horns in the relatively small space of the roof. It provided a welcome change from the normal pastime activities that occupied the long, hot summers, one of which was catching a wasp. They would squeeze the sting out of the end of its abdomen, attach a short piece of cotton string to one of its eight legs, and fly it in circles, till the wasp exhausted itself and died, or its leg became detached from its body, and it flew away. A similar game was played with locusts, with the added advantage that locusts had no sting to be removed.

The day came when the ram had to be slaughtered. A rabbi was present to ensure that the slaughter took place in accordance with Jewish kosher rules, not that that made any difference to the unfortunate creature. The boys looked on as their playmate for the past seven days had its throat cut by a square-shouldered, short, stocky butcher with a large protective apron. Blood squirted all over the stone floor of the courtyard, as the beast wiggled and wriggled and jerked. Its struggle ceased only when the last drop of blood left its body, with an audible 'blob' on the blood-covered floor. The butcher let go and, using a sharp, short knife, made an incision in the neck under the dead animal's skin. He then placed his mouth on the opening he created, took in a large breath of air, and with cheeks swelling to their extremities, and face turning red then crimson, he exhaled into the gap with great force. This was repeated several times. The ram began to inflate and expand outwards like a plastic balloon, larger and larger, as the air penetrated the gap between skin and flesh. The younger siblings began to think their ram might begin to float. The butcher suddenly stopped and, out of breath, inspected his work, and found it satisfactory enough to stop pumping air into the puffed-up beast and start to peel off the skin using his trusted sharp knife, which he sharpened on a leather razor strop at regular intervals. A carcass covered with a thin layer of fat was revealed – what was but a couple of minutes before a live, kicking animal. The boys looked on. They could refuse to eat their friend, but they remembered what happened the last time they went on hunger strike.

It was a year or so ago when Um-Kamal and her husband decided on a cull of the pigeons that were quickly exceeding the capacity of the cage that Abu-Kamal had built on the roof. A dozen pigeons were chosen for slaughter, to be a substitute for the chicken in the traditional *tebit*, the chicken-and-rice dish that was kept overnight on a slow flame on Friday evening to meet the Jewish obligation of not cooking on the Sabbath. The food smelled delicious, and looked appetizing, but the younger children could not eat what had been only a couple of days ago their pets. Each pigeon in the pot had a name that Layla had given it, reflecting its character and general demeanour. They refused to eat them. They looked on as the rest of the family enjoyed the dark breast meat of the pigeons, the gravy, and the accompanying orange-coloured, pigeon-flavoured rice. Um-Kamal tried to tempt them with a sweet. Abu-Kamal threatened them. They sat at the bottom of the staircase and refused to budge.

'Okay,' said Rosette, 'if you don't want to eat, don't eat.' A few hours later, with stomachs empty and bodies yearning for sustenance, the youngest gave in first. He was soon followed by the others, as they began to eat their beloved pets.

8

Ezra's quest

THE LAST THING Um-Kamal wanted was for Ezra, her second eldest son, to join the exodus of Jews from Iraq. The family had decided to stay. They couldn't abandon Sasson. It's one thing to have one son in prison; at least she could visit him, albeit only twice a year. Going to Israel was quite different. She may not see him or hear from him ever again.

But Ezra's future prospects in Iraq were abruptly thrown into doubt when he failed to get a place at Baghdad University to do engineering, in spite of the fact that he had some of the highest marks in the national baccalaureate. In that year, although there was no law forbidding Jews from entering university, no Jew managed to get a place. Jewish organizations approached the Minister of Education. He was sympathetic, but could not directly interfere. He told them to choose someone eligible and send him to the university and 'we'll see what we can do'. The organizations representing the Jewish community, eager to fight anti-Jewish hostilities (unlike their Zionist counterparts who thrived on them), were determined to put this to the test. They looked at the baccalaureate results of all Jews that sat the exams that year, and they selected Ezra. His marks were some of the highest in the whole of Iraq: 96% in physics, 95% in trigonometry, 94% in geometry and 93% in English. He was to be a test case. On his young shoulders lay the future of the Jews in Iraq, or so he and they perceived the situation. The Chief Rabbi, a short man with broad shoulders and a long, thick, white beard, eager to show the Jewish community that he was doing something to protect them, told Ezra to go to see the Jewish member of the *Majlis*, Senator Menahem Daniel.

Ezra arrived at the big house on the Tigris, and pulled the handle hanging on a chain on the side of the iron gate. He noticed the high wall surrounding the house, with its barbed wire stretching above it. He waited, and just as he was about to pull the handle down again, the gate swung open revealing a stone path lined with lemon trees, which led to an imposing dark oak double door.

'Come in. His Excellency is expecting you,' said a decently dressed young man, who spoke with a Muslim accent, whom Ezra assumed to be a servant, but who turned out to be the Senator's secretary. A large bullmastiff guard dog stood at the entrance, alert, watching. It snarled, and Ezra halted his step. The secretary yelled at the creature in English. The dog retreated, turned around, and went into the house. Ezra followed.

'*Ahlan, ahlan*,' said the Senator's wife when Ezra stepped onto the marble floor of the circular courtyard. She was a woman in her late thirties, with a Western style of dress, wearing yellow high-heeled shoes, with a couple of gold bangles adorning her left wrist, another on her right, and a rather large gold brooch, depicting Hammurabi handing out his Babylonian code to a high priest, which was pinned on her bright yellow blouse.

'Come, come in,' she said, pointing to a door leading to the lounge. 'Sit down.'

Ezra sank into a large plush armchair covered with a grey sheepskin. The room was luxurious, with two large leather sofas, several crimson and black armchairs, and a large glass-topped round coffee table, adorned with a massive bunch of flowers, and placed under a glistening crystal chandelier hanging from a high ceiling. There were sweets, seeds and nuts placed randomly on various small tables scattered around the room. A servant came with Turkish coffee in a porcelain Mirra cup, with delicate gilded decorations. Not accustomed to drinking Turkish coffee, Ezra sipped it awkwardly. The Senator, dressed in a white suit with abundant black hair brushed back from his face, suddenly entered the lounge from a door at the far end of the room, making Ezra jump to his feet. The Senator took this as a mark of respect, and gestured for Ezra to remain seated in the manner of someone used to people standing when he enters a room. Ezra resumed his sitting position. The Senator was a large overweight man with a belly hanging over his leather belt, fifteen or more years his wife's senior, and clean shaven except for the compulsory moustache. He parked his large posterior on an armchair next to Ezra, leaned back and said, 'So, you're the genius boy. You're going to be our test case. Are you up for it?' Without waiting for a reply, he said, 'Show me your certificate.'

Ezra handed over the baccalaureate certificate that he had neatly folded inside his back pocket.

'Ninety-five, ninety-three, ninety... What school did you go to?' asked the Senator.

'Shamash Secondary.'

'In Qamber Ali?' exclaimed the Senator.

'Yes, sir,' said Ezra.

'And your brother, Kamal, he is studying medicine. He also went to the same school?'

Ezra nodded.

'That's a great achievement,' said the Senator, nodding. 'Maybe I should've sent my son there instead of the American Academy.'

He looked up to the ceiling, and recalled that he himself had only managed 75% in his exams. 'But that was during the Ottoman rule, well before you were born, a long time ago.'

He looked directly into Ezra's eyes. 'We need young people like you. You hold the future of Iraq in your hands. The Minister said he wants to see you.'

'What? *El-Wazir?*' interrupted Ezra.

'I talked to him,' said the Senator. 'He was a friend of my father. They did business together.'

The Senator went to the door and called his secretary. He turned around to Ezra and said, 'The British and the Americans are agitating. Scores of young Jews are being encouraged to escape to Iran, and then fly to Israel. It was a shock to all of us – that vote at the United Nations, and Russia voting for it! I blame Stalin. Jews, communist Jews, are now in prison because of him, and they wouldn't have a word said against him. Your brother is one of them, isn't he?'

Ezra nodded.

'How many years did he get?'

'Eight years.'

'He's lucky. Most got ten or more,' said the Senator.

He examined the certificate again, as if to make sure that what he saw the first time was real.

'If marks like these don't get you into university, it'll be proof that Jews have no future in Iraq. *El-Wazir* knows that, and he wants to do something about it. He is sticking his neck out, like the rest of us. If Nuri Al-Said comes back, he'll be accused of communist sympathies, and that will be the end of him. They say Israel is home for the Jews! But we have a home. For 2,700 years, this has been our home.'

With a deep sigh, he went on, as if talking to himself. 'What the Zionists want, the Zionists get.'

The secretary entered the room with a folder and a gold-plated Parker fountain pen in his hand.

'Take down a letter to the Minister of Education. Your Excellency...' began the Senator.

When he had finished, the Senator read the letter carefully, signed it, folded it, and inserted it into an envelope that had a prominent House of Senate red emblem on the right-hand corner. The secretary carefully sealed it.

'Take this to *el-Wazir* tomorrow,' said the Senator handing the letter to Ezra.

Ezra was taken aback. No one saw the Minister, certainly not a kid from Qamber Ali.

The next day, Ezra left for the Ministry of Education on the much-repaired, much-treasured, family bicycle.

It was almost 11 o'clock when he reached the Ministry of Education, sweating, having cycled all the way from Qamber Ali. It must have been 40 degrees and rising; so hot that even the wild pigeons and brown sparrows were hiding among the branches of the only tree in the vicinity, gasping for air. The only other soul was a disgruntled, malnourished donkey with bones protruding from its hind legs, ridden by a teenager in a worn-out traditional dishdasha of indiscernible colour, who kept encouraging the unfortunate animal to move by way of a constant stream of blows to its backside with the thick end of a tree branch, causing the skin of the beast to bleed. The blows did not seem to change the behaviour of the beast, for it continued to put one hoof in front of the other in the unhurried manner that is a speciality of donkeys. For his part, the teenager was administering the blows in a regular rhythm that bore no relation to the reluctance of the beleaguered creature to move or otherwise. Ezra wondered what would happen if the animal were treated more humanely; but humanity was in short supply in these hellishly hot days of Baghdad.

Ezra got off the bike and leaned against the trunk of the tree to cool down before he approached the Ministry. A sentry – a soldier with an ill-fitting, fading uniform and an old First World War rifle over his shoulder – stood guard at the entrance. Upon seeing Ezra, the soldier stood straight, and looked menacingly at him.

'I'm here to see his Excellency *el-Wazir*,' said Ezra.

'And who else do you want to see, the King maybe?'

'I have a personal letter from his Excellency, Senator...'

The guard stretched out his hand. 'Here, let me see.'

'You can't open it. It's personal for *el-Wazir*.'

The sentry, seeing the House of Senate emblem, returned it and opened the gate.

The Minister, sitting back on a chair behind a huge desk, with one black Bakelite telephone receiver on his right, a couple of folders to his left, weighed down by a diamond-studded paperweight in the shape of a tiger, twirled his moustache and sipped cold tea. Hanging on the wall behind him were two large black and white portraits of the young King Faisal, who inherited the throne at the age of five when his father was killed in a mysterious car crash in 1939, and the King's regent, Crown Prince Abdullah. He looked at the letter, smiled, and said, 'As you know, we are a civilized country and honourable people. There is no law that prohibits Jews from taking up advanced courses at our universities.'

He folded the letter. 'We have Jewish girls at university. Your sister is one. What is she studying?'

'Medicine, your Excellency.'

'Medicine! She wants to be a doctor. We need doctors, we need engineers.' The Minister picked up a small handful of chick peas and offered some to Ezra, but he declined.

'Have you been to Rome?' asked the Minister.

Ezra shook his head, with a barely audible 'No'.

'When I was in Rome, I went to a small church, the Basilica di Santa Pudenziana,' said *el-Wazir*, pronouncing the name with a perfect Italian accent. 'It has a mosaic, the mosaic of Santa Pudenziana. That mosaic is 1,500 years old, and it looked pristine. Every six months, it is cleaned and inspected for any damage. Iraq is a mosaic, a beautiful intricate mosaic; every piece is different. By itself, each piece is insignificant – but when they are assembled, you have a masterpiece. If a piece is damaged, even if the smallest piece is damaged or removed, the mosaic is impaired, disabled, weakened. The Italians look after their mosaics, but we allow the foreigner to trample all over ours, and ours is older; 1,000 years older.' He looked at Ezra. 'What do you think?'

'I'm not political. I keep away from politics.'

'This is Iraq,' said *el-Wazir*. 'Everyone is political, even ten-year-olds are political.'

'I just want to study engineering and serve the King and country.'

'Oh, yes, serve the King and country.' *El-Wazir* half turned and looked at the two portraits behind him. 'The King and his uncle do a lot for us.'

'They do indeed; they do everything for us.'

'Well said, well said, young Jew. Now, tell me, have you been to see the Dean of the University for Engineering?'

'Yes, I have.'

'And…?'

'He said he can't offer me a place.'

'Why? Did he say why?'

'No,' said Ezra, 'he didn't give me any reason.'

'Go and see him.'

'But I've already been to see him.'

'Go and see him again; and this time tell him I sent you.'

'Couldn't you give me a letter or something?' said Ezra.

'We live in dangerous times young Jew. I can't be seen to interfere. Go and see him. I'm sure he'll do the right thing.'

The Dean, sitting behind a grand oak desk, opened a file stamped JEWS in large black letters, and inspected its contents. 'We can't offer you a place at our university,' he said.

'His Excellency, *el-Wazir*, thought you could reconsider.'

The Dean casually flipped through the paperwork in front of him. 'I have reconsidered the matter. I'm afraid I can't offer you a place.'

'Is it because I'm a Jew? Because there is no law–'

'Don't be impertinent, and don't lecture me about the law.'

'I'm not–.'

'No, it's not because you are a Jew. You Jews, you think everything is about you; the whole world revolves around you. Have some humility and some respect. There are other reasons why I can't offer you a place at my university.'

He closed the file, lifted a paperweight, and deliberately placed the file at the bottom of the pile, returning the paperweight to its resting place. He looked at Ezra with cold, menacing eyes.

'How discourteous! How ungrateful! After all this country has done for you. Get out, get out before I call the police and get you arrested for insolence and for disrespecting the King.'

The next day, Ezra went to the local synagogue and added his name to the ever-lengthening list of Jews who wished to leave.

9

Two weeks later

THE JOURNEY TO Nigret al-Salman was long and arduous. Situated in the middle of the desert, Nigret al-Salman was a British army citadel turned into a prison for political prisoners, mostly communists. It was the negative image of South Africa's infamous Robben Island prison – a prison surrounded by sand. Um-Kamal was joined by Ezra who, having been refused a university place to study engineering, reluctantly joined the thousands of Jews who signed away their Iraqi nationality in order to immigrate to Israel.

This was his only opportunity to see his brother before he was due to leave in a couple of weeks. Um-Kamal also took her younger son with her, ten-year-old Sa'id. A young child accorded a motherly respectability to a woman, eliciting a softer approach from the authorities. Also on the journey were some fifty or so mothers and sisters and a handful of fathers and brothers of the inmates. They took a train from Baghdad to the nearest town, Al-Samawah. From there they boarded three ageing, wooden-framed coaches for the remaining 120 miles through the desert to the infamous prison. On later occasions, Abu-Kamal accompanied her on the train journey, but stayed in Al-Samawah. He could not face the prospect of seeing his son in prison.

It was early afternoon, and having informed the *Hagannah*, the desert police, of their destination, they were on their way. The desert police had to be informed every time anyone attempted a journey into the desert.

A rare storm had visited the area, and a lot of rain had fallen on the dry sand the night before, but that didn't deter the convoy. The lead driver, with his guide sitting next to him, pressed the ignition button. The engine reluctantly and slowly turned, the large exhaust pipe that stretched up to the roof of the coach began to vibrate violently, puffing black fumes into the clean air, before the engine settled into a regular rhythm – a rhythm typical of 1940s petrol-driven trucks and lorries: a short-lived burst of 'vroom' that peters out almost completely, only to be followed by another burst of 'vroom' that brings it back to life, shaking the wooden frame, and with it its load of luggage and human souls. The gears were forcibly thrust into first, making a crunching sound. The vehicle jerked forward, the sudden shudder startling the passengers. There was a sharp intake of breath from the women. The drivers of the other two coaches followed suit. They were on their way, guided by nothing other than the sun in the day, and the stars at night. There was no identifiable track, let alone a road, out into the desert, no arrow pointing to their destination. The desert prison camp where hundreds had been imprisoned, and tortured, and some had perished, was located in the small enclave of Al-Salman, south of Al-Samawah, itself 240 miles south-east of Baghdad.

The three coaches travelled in a convoy; not in line, but abreast, to avoid the sand propelled by the large Goodyear tyres as they tore into the virgin sand. The desert was flat, with a few featureless dunes on the horizon. A mirage of flowing water could be seen in the distance. Um-Kamal was appropriately dressed in the traditional black abaya, covering all of her body except for the face – a type of armour made of soft fabric that isolated women from the outside world. The abaya came into its own in these conditions, providing protection against the wind that kept up a constant biting stream of tiny particles blasting through the coach and settling randomly inside the vehicle, forming a thin pale-brown layer that covered everything. Anyone who sat near a window would have immediately understood why glass, whose main constituent is sand, is so sharp when broken.

The sun, once it decided that the day was up, quickly disappeared over the horizon in an orgy of yellow, orange and red that engulfed the sky to their left. As darkness fell, the only guide through the desert was the stars, and there were millions of them. After driving for a while, the lead coach stopped and the guide, who sat next to the driver, sharing a cigarette, got out. Ezra, who was seated just behind the driver, took the opportunity to stretch his legs and followed him out. The guide looked up to the heavens, and Ezra did the same. The sky was like a tapestry of bright and not-so-bright singularities of light. The guide turned around and looked back from whence the coach had come. Ezra had a sinking feeling that they were travelling in the wrong direction. The guide then examined the lower part of the sky to his left at some length and, having identified what he was looking for, the group of seven stars in the shape of a plough, he moved his head along the line made by joining the two pointer stars that form the handle of the plough, which took him to the North Star. Ezra copied the guide's movements, and could clearly identify the bright star that sits directly above the North Pole. The guide made a 90-degree turn to his left and, with unwarranted confidence, stretched out his right arm and triumphantly called out, 'This way.' Ezra quickly climbed back into his seat, followed by the guide, who was not too pleased that a passenger should intrude into his personal space when he was busy trying to guide the coach safely to its destination. There was no moon, and the feeble headlights gave no clue of what lay ahead; there was nothing to reflect the light back, except for the pale sand that stretched forever.

Not long after, the convoy began to hit pockets of mud that had not completely dried out from the rain that had visited the desert, making it difficult for the wheels to get traction, with the vehicles slipping and sliding this way and that, as the balding Goodyear tyres attempted to get a grip. The appearance of these mud pockets was decidedly unpredictable and, following a particularly scary slide, with the driver losing control of the coach and almost turning over, the driver and the guide of the lead coach decided not to continue the journey and to camp down for the night. They signalled to the other drivers to start forming a semi-circle on a patch of sand.

The canopy of stars provided a faint glow, allowing the travellers to see without the need for artificial light. A fire was lit, and coffee was made and shared. The guide, having finished his cup of strong Turkish coffee, lifted his right hand and placed it against his right cheek, leaned slightly to the right and let out the haunting notes '*Yalayli, yalaylati... yalayla a ah*'. This was the overture that preceded traditional ballads. Like the gasps of a liberated soul, they pierced the tranquillity of the desert and disappeared into the distant air, like a dazzling freshwater pearl drifting along the bottom of a gentle stream, never to be seen again. He sang a lament about a young man who, having ridden his camel all day in pursuit of his love, arrived at an inn, only to be told by the innkeeper that the love he was seeking had been there, but had left early that morning.

The temperature fell dramatically. One by one, the travellers fell asleep, fully clothed, covered with whatever they happened to have by way of blankets and robes.

When Ezra opened his eyes, Um-Kamal was already up, washing her face and folding the thin blanket that she slept under. Through the early, thin mist that hovered above the sand, he could see the silhouettes of two camels, one lying down and munching – whatever it is that camels munch, even when there is nothing obvious in their vicinity that could be remotely considered suitable for munching – and a second camel standing, snorting. Behind them, he could just make out human shapes under the brown canvas of a tent.

'Look,' Ezra called to Sa'id, prodding him with the forefinger of his right hand, 'just like a scene from the Arabian Nights.'

The shy, early sun rays roused the sleeping travellers and they began to stir, with each one engaged in the early morning rituals of rubbing eyes, wiping faces, scratching heads, coughing, and clearing nostrils of accumulated dust.

'You can ask them for some milk,' said the driver, pointing to the Bedouin tent. He sensed Sa'id's desire for some breakfast. Sa'id looked to his mother for approval, and she gestured to Ezra to accompany him.

'But don't offend them by offering money. That will be considered an unforgivable insult,' advised the driver, as he moved on to ensure that everyone was up and ready to resume the journey before the sun got hold of the sky.

The camels weren't in the pristine condition that their silhouettes had suggested. They were dishevelled and dirty, with small humps that bent over at the top, and they grunted and sneezed. One spat at Sa'id as he approached. Ezra took his little brother's hand and led him the long way around towards the tent, which now looked larger and more spacious, with a dirty brown camel-hair carpet adorning its floor. There was nothing remotely comparable to the images conjured up by the stories Scheherazade told her king. The only colour other than brown was provided by a magnificent hawk with red and gold feathers who perched on a makeshift stand, looking dejected, with her head in a hood, preventing her from seeing and reacting.

A tall, thin, heavily bearded man with a black-striped head dress and flowing fading-white robe, spoke through three missing front teeth, in perfect, classical Arabic. 'Welcome. Come, come. Would you like some milk, or perhaps some *geymer*, some cream?'

'Yes, please,' replied the two brothers almost in unison. The tall man poured some milk from a goat skin into the jug Ezra was holding, and placed a slice of delicious-looking *geymer* in Sa'id's outstretched hands. With 'don't offend them by offering money' ringing in their ears, they thanked him, said goodbye, and walked back. It was an encounter that was to be told countless times over dinner tables for years to come.

Um-Kamal's family were the last to get on the lead coach. The driver, Hassan, kept up a constant stream of encouraging words, urging the travellers to get in the coach as quickly as possible.

With the sun behind them, the driver pressed the ignition switch. The engine rumbled for a while, reluctant to leave its slumber, only to wake up with a shake and a harsh 'vroom'. The driver drew heavily on the cigarette between his lips, handed it to the guide who was seated next to him and, exhaling a jet of white smoke that expanded to fill the space between him and the windscreen, engaged first gear with a clunk and, with the passengers tensing their muscles at the expectation of the inevitable wrench, pulled the clutch. The jerk, though expected, still triggered a loud 'Ooh' from the women, who by now had pulled their abayas over their faces in anticipation of the wind and dust that was to follow once the coach began to move.

The weary travellers tried various tactics to keep cool, which invariably failed, and inevitably resulted in one woman suddenly bending over and fainting. Women didn't have the privilege the men had of baring their heads, loosening their shirts, and stretching their legs. Traditional humility prevented them from escaping their all-encompassing shroud. One or two men stood with their heads bent to avoid touching the hot roof cleared some space, and nearby children shifted to provide some comfort for the fainted woman. She was sprayed with water, and fanned with whatever was at hand, from a piece of cardboard to the end of a head scarf.

When the outline of the reddish-brown outer perimeter of the prison compound finally appeared in the distance, there was an audible release of tension, with the travellers shifting and straining to get a better view. They had been driving under the bright orange sun for six hours, stopping from time to time for the guide to get out to examine the shadow that the sun threw on the ground and, taking account of the position of the sun in the sky, set the direction for the lead driver to take.

The coaches finally came to a stop. The travellers stepped out, like newly formed butterflies popping out of their chrysalises. The drivers were busy untying the ropes that held the parcels, boxes and other luggage to the roofs of the coaches. They gently took them down and placed them on the hot, bare ground in a tidy line.

The citadel, built by the British as a garrison during their various expeditions in Mesopotamia, looked more benign than expected for such an infamous prison, from which not a single prisoner had ever escaped. Remarkably, its perimeter walls were no higher than 6 or 7 feet.

The visitors were confronted with a dozen scruffy-looking military-type prison guards in pale khaki military-style uniforms that were either one size too small or one size too large. The guards stood in two rows; a front row with sticks in their hands, and a second row with rifles pointing haphazardly in the direction of the visitors. If they were to be fired, the gun shots would more likely hit the backs of the heads of the guards in the front row than any intended targets.

The Prison Governor was a short man, immaculately dressed in a snug-fitting, blue uniform and a white peaked cap, with a thin moustache that extended far beyond the two corners of his mouth. He carried a handgun in a holster on his right hip, and a thin black leather cane in his left hand. He spoke little, preferring to issue orders with subtle movements of his cane, head, and sometimes eyebrows.

The visitors were herded by the stick-waving guards into two groups. Ezra and the other men were taken behind the stationary coaches, which had steam puffing out of their open hoods. They were roughly and unceremoniously searched. The women and children were shepherded into a line in front of the coaches, and though human sensibilities were suspended in this godforsaken place, centuries-old traditions decreeing that a man must not come within touching distance of a woman, let alone actually touch her, were observed. The women were not searched. There were no women among the prison guards.

The parcels, sacks, boxes, jugs, and jars the visitors brought their loved ones were thoroughly inspected. Jars were emptied, jugs broken, and sacks slashed. Rice mingled with dried tomato paste, apricot jam with date syrup. Not much food could be salvaged. Um-Kamal looked on, her arms firmly folded against her chest under her abaya.

A nod from the Governor, and a stick-waving guard with an extra stripe on his shoulder pad announced that none of the men would be allowed in. Ezra and the other men were ordered to stand against the perimeter wall. The sun had just passed its peak, so there was no shade. It did not escape Ezra's notice that under the early afternoon sun, the guards were suffering as much, if not more, under their heavy uniforms. He wondered if being sent to this hellhole was as much a punishment for them as it was for the prisoners.

One by one, the women and children were herded through a small gate, up a few steps, and down again through an arched, short passage, and into the prison yard – which was crossed by two diagonal paved pathways – a spacious, bare ground that had served as a parade ground for the British army.

The prisoners were sitting on straw mats that were scattered at random in the yard. In contrast to the anxious and tearful faces of the women, the prisoners were delighted to see their relatives and, when they recognized them, they smiled broadly. They made a lot of fuss of the children that accompanied the women, playfully laughing and joking with them, regardless of whether they were related to them or not. Um-Kamal found Sasson sitting with another prisoner at the far end of the yard and, holding Sa'id's hand, she walked firmly to sit next to him. Sa'id wondered why his mother, even before she uttered a single word, stretched out her arm to feel both of Sasson's ankles that were invisible under the long prison-issue pyjamas. The answer was not long in coming, for the prisoner squatting next to his brother – a jolly, red-faced, strong-looking, stocky man in his thirties – had hefty iron foot shackles on both ankles connected to a chain that stretched up both of his legs, all the way around his neck and back, over his arms to his wrists. He didn't seem to be unduly perturbed by his elaborate shackles, but moved and chatted amicably, making a big fuss of Sa'id. But for the chain-smoking armed guards leisurely strolling up and down the paved pathways, one could have easily mistaken the scene for a pleasant family day out.

Sasson put his right arm around Sa'id's shoulders and squeezed him hard. Sa'id looked at him with admiration. Um-Kamal, holding Sasson's left hand, looked at his face and with moist eyes whispered, 'You are so thin.' She was determined not to let him see her crying.

'Did they torture you?' she asked.

'No,' said Sasson.

'But you are so thin.'

'Don't worry. I'm in perfect health,' said Sasson. Looking at the other prisoner, he chuckled and added, 'They look after us here.'

The red-faced prisoner suddenly interrupted the conversation he was having with his wife, who was telling him of their two young girls and how well they were doing at school. Turning to Um-Kamal, just as a prison guard passed by, he said in a quiet voice, 'Convey my regards to my uncle.'

Um-Kamal was startled, her heart skipped a beat. That was the code she had been told to listen out for. She quickly composed herself and replied, 'Abu-Ahmad says hello,' and immediately released the cloth strap that was holding the three small parcels to her chest. The parcels fell under her dress to rest in her lap. She surreptitiously eased them out, one by one, and slipped one to Sasson, who grabbed it and swiftly tucked it under his pyjama top, and the other two to the red-faced prisoner, who casually continued his conversation with his wife.

Turning to Um-Kamal, the red-faced prisoner said, 'Send my regards to my uncle, and give him this.' He handed her a brown paper bag, half full of nuts, in full view of a passing prison guard. 'I saved them especially for him.'

The prison guard triumphantly seized the brown paper bag. 'What is this? Trying to smuggle prohibited literature?'

'Just a present for my uncle,' said the red-faced prisoner.

The guard examined the contents closely, picked out one of the nuts, placed it in his mouth, and crushed it with his few remaining teeth. He then emptied half of the contents into his pocket and handed the paper bag back to Um-Kamal, who was more mystified by the exchange than the guard himself was.

'Can I have one?' asked Sa'id.

'No! Not for you,' Um-Kamal rebuked him.

'Take good care of it,' said the red-faced prisoner to Um-Kamal.

Um-Kamal folded the top of the paper bag and placed it carefully inside her woven handbag, tucking it under her abaya.

Back at home, Um-Kamal emptied the brown paper bag onto the dinner table and carefully examined it. There was nothing out of the ordinary about it, just a perfectly normal brown paper bag, but she knew it contained a secret compartment, some message, some document – but where, and how?

'I got a present for you,' said Um-Kamal, when Mohamed Saleh opened the front door of his house in a narrow alleyway, not far from where she lived. Mohamed wiped his face with the towel he was carrying in his hand, put his spectacles on and, when he recognized Um-Kamal, smiled and said, 'Um-Kamal, *marhaba, marhaba*, come in.'

'I got a present for you,' she repeated, and she handed the empty brown paper bag over to him.

'I was expecting this. What kept you?'

'I didn't want to make it obvious, just in case I was being watched.'

He took the paper bag, folded it and put it in his pocket. 'A cup of chai?'

'No, *shukran*,' she replied. 'What is so important about this bag? I examined it, and it's empty. There is nothing there.'

'Um-Kamal! But there is. I will show you.'

Mohamed put a saucepan on the kerosene stove and when the water started to vaporize, he placed the paper bag above the rising steam and gradually began to prise open one of the sealed edges with a flick knife he got out of his pocket. Um-Kamal suddenly realized that the sealed ends of the paper bag were slightly bulkier than they needed to be, given the thin paper used to make the bag. Gradually, the sealed edges became moist and began to give way, aided by the skilful manipulation of the sharp knife. When the edges were completely open, Mohamed pulled out an immaculately folded, light-brown piece of paper with tiny writing on both sides. Two more pages were retrieved from the other two edges. He picked up a magnifying glass from a drawer and used it to examine one of the pages.

'We'll have this out immediately. It's dynamite.'

As Um-Kamal turned to leave, Mohamed said, 'When is your next visit comrade?'

Um-Kamal turned back, placed both hands on his bare arms and said, 'I'm not a comrade, just an ordinary woman, a mother.' On the doorstep, she turned again and said, 'In six months' time. We are only allowed two visits a year.'

'Come and see me before you go,' he said.

It suddenly dawned on Um-Kamal – unwittingly she had become a courier for the Communist Party.

10

Letter from Israel, via India

'UM-KAMAL, UM-KAMAL!' shouted the postman through the small gap in the front door. 'Um-Kamal, you have a letter from Bombay, from India.'

Um-Kamal threw her abaya over her shoulders and rushed to the door. 'Bless you.' She took the letter and said, 'Wait there.'

She went back to the main room, and then returned. 'Here, bless you,' she said, giving him 200 fils. 'Next time you bring me a letter from India, you'll have a quarter of a dinar.'

Um-Kamal looked at the letter for a while before opening it. There was another envelope inside, with different stamps on its top-right corner. She placed it against the clock on the shelf and sat down staring at it. She wondered what was inside it, what story it would tell. With no political recognition between Israel and neighbouring Arab countries, the letter had to take a convoluted route. It came via some acquaintances they knew in Bombay, who agreed to forward letters from Israel. This was his second letter. In his earlier letter, Ezra talked about the conditions that immigrants from Arab countries to Israel had to face. The welcome to the new country was unexpectedly harsh. Immediately upon landing, Ezra had been sprayed with a toxic DDI compound, which was the forerunner to DDT, and then sent to live in a temporary tent camp with the other immigrants from the Middle East. The Israeli government regarded those who came from Arab countries as disease-ridden, dirty and uncivilized, and looked down on them, treating them with disdain and contempt. Ezra mused that he was a second-class citizen in Iraq for being a Jew, and a second-class citizen in a Jewish state for being Iraqi.

Is he okay? Um-Kamal wondered; how hard has it been for him? The first letter came shortly after he had left, but it failed to mention that he almost didn't make the plane.

A coach took fifty or so Jews, mostly families with young and not-so-young children to the airport, where a plane was waiting to take them on their journey out of Iraq. They were crammed in a holding area with their one suitcase each, holding their one-departure permits, waiting for their papers to be stamped before climbing into the propeller-driven plane, which they could see through the large glass window. Ezra looked around. He could see the concourse where those seeing off the travellers gathered. There was no sign of any of his family. The only person he could recognize was Abraham El-Fannan, an old school friend who had come to see him off.

A police officer in plain clothes entered the holding area and, after exchanging a few words with the two policemen guarding the would-be passengers, pushed his way through the compressed mass of nervous people, avoiding the multitude of suitcases in the middle, and called for silence. The noisy, animated conversations mingled with the noise of crying babies. He tried again, with a similar level of success.

'Quiet! Quiet!' he shouted, followed by indecipherable shouts from the two guards at the door.

Silence descended. The only noise was of a baby crying; faces full of fear and anxiety turned to whence the call for silence had come. The officer slowly and deliberately took a monocle out of his jacket pocket, tucked it neatly against his left eye and, reading from a paper he held in his right hand, called out two names; one was Ezra's: 'Ezra Maude Abraham.' It was followed by another name, that of a Zionist whom Ezra knew from school. Ezra reluctantly raised his arm, as did the Zionist friend.

'Ah!' exclaimed the officer. Turning to the two guards, he said, 'Take them away.'

Ezra's blood seemed to drain away; his face turned pale. He had a sinking feeling in his stomach. The other passengers looked on with obvious relief that it wasn't them. The Zionist attempted to make a run for it, stumbling on the suitcases that littered the floor in the process, but there was nowhere to run; it was a futile gesture. The two guards moved quickly and, as they held him roughly by the arm, he grabbed the leather handle of his suitcase. The officer, calmly watching the proceedings, shouted, 'Leave it! You can't take it with you.'

The two Jews were taken to a waiting police car, which drove at considerable speed, with sirens blaring, to Baghdad's CID headquarters, an imposing three-storey building with narrow, long windows and a frightening reputation. Beatings and torture were routine. They were marched into a large room, with a window with vertical metal bars on the left, and a heavy wooden door inscribed with CID CHIEF in large letters on the right.

A constable with pronounced black hair sprouting out of his left nostril gave Ezra a hard slap on the back of the neck, so hard that another constable said '*Yarham jidick*, God bless your grandfather, well done,' in the manner of someone praising a tennis player on a well-executed backhand.

The two detainees sat and waited; they had no food and no water, and if they wanted to go to the toilet they had to be accompanied.

Suddenly, the three policemen guarding them stood to attention, as an officer in an immaculate light-blue uniform, with the *Mukhabarat* insignia on the left lapel and a large pair of spectacles resting on his pointed nose, walked in. They stood. The policemen saluted:

'Sir!'

The enthusiastic constable opened the door with the CID CHIEF inscription and, standing to attention, held it open, as the officer walked in without saying a word.

The Zionist went in first; it wasn't long before he was brought out. The constable who had given Ezra that commendable slap on the back of the neck was beating the Zionist on the face, on the back, and on the neck. He was joined by the other two, who took pleasure in kicking his legs, making him stumble and fall, giving them a good opportunity to kick him in the guts. He was taken down to the cellars. Ezra could hear him scream; his screams gradually faded away.

Ezra feared the worst. 'This is the end,' he thought.

When the policemen finally came back, they were breathing heavily; beatings are hard work for both sides of the equation. Ezra was called in.

The CID Chief sat at a large desk with metal legs and leather top, a telephone to his right and a table lamp to his left; he had Ezra's passport and a few papers in front of him; three policemen, including the enthusiastic constable, stood by.

As soon as Ezra entered the room, the CID Chief, with a whimsical smile, looked at him and said, 'Do you know what *khavere* is?'

'I don't know what *khavier* is,' replied Ezra.

'Ah, you don't know the meaning of *khavere*, but you can pronounce it properly; better than me.'

'Oh, *khavier*. Yes, yes, I do know what *khavier* is.'

'What does it mean?'

'It is Hebrew for "friend".'

'Ah, Hebrew! Why lie then? Don't you know the saying, "*hakika munjat*" – "truth pays"?'

Ezra felt forlorn, desperate. He was angry that it would all end like this. He didn't care anymore; he had nothing to lose. He might as well tell the truth; go down with his dignity and integrity intact. He refused to grovel and beg.

'Sorry. You took me by surprise. I'll tell you the truth. I'll tell it straight from now on.'

The CID Chief leant back on his leather armchair.

'How do you know Hebrew?'

'Because I studied it.'

'And why did you study Hebrew?'

'Because I'm going to Israel.'

To the discerning ear, a clear shifting of feet by the constables could clearly be heard, as clearly as their thoughts; this Jew is really in for it. Even a casual mention of Israel would elicit immediate retribution, let alone admitting a wish to go there. They began to psych themselves for another beating.

The CID officer showed Ezra a piece of paper with a long list of names. He pointed to one of the names, and asked Ezra if it was him. Ezra said, 'Yes.'

'Is this your address?'

'Yes.'

'Your father's name, family name?'

'Yes, yes…'

The officer looked puzzled; why would anyone incriminate himself in this way? It was not logical.

The officer held up the sheet of paper and said, 'Do you know what this is?'

'No.'

Ezra didn't use the word 'Sir'. Throughout all of the interrogation, he never addressed the officer as Sir. Everyone else did: 'Sir this', 'Sir that'; 'Yes Sir', 'No Sir'. He didn't.

'This is a list of wanted Zionists; Zionist agitators and conspirators.'

'What has this got to do with me?'

'How is it that your name is on this list?'

'*Ma 'adri*, I don't know,' Ezra shouted. 'How do I know? *Ma 'adri, ma 'adri.*'

The CID Chief paused for what, to Ezra, seemed a very long time. He saw himself as a civilized detective, a cut above the corrupt mob that ran the police force. He was seeking the truth. Before beating someone up, he wanted to make sure it was the right person, and then he'd order a beating. He held Ezra's passport in his hand; there was silence; no one dared to breathe; after ten seconds, in almost a whisper, he said, 'Take him to the airport.'

Ezra thought it was a dream. He twisted the forefinger of his right hand as hard as he could. He sank his left thumbnail into his bare right arm. It hurt, and blood began to seep from the area. He wasn't dreaming.

'Sir, the plane has long gone, Sir,' said one of the policemen.

'Take him anyway, and keep him there overnight.'

'What shall we take him in, Sir?'

'In a car, a police car.'

'We don't have a car, Sir.'

'What? What do you mean, we don't have a car?'

'We have only one car, Sir; and it's in Betawaniya, Sir.'

'Get another car?'

'Sir, the only other car we have is in the garage being repaired, Sir.'

The officer was incensed.

'What? We have one vehicle only? All of Baghdad, and we only have one car? Go and get a car here immediately!'

It was surreal; like one of those plays where a hostage is forgotten in the midst of arguments among his abductors; it was as if Ezra was a mere unconcerned bystander. And like a helpful bystander, he said, 'Can we take a taxi?'

'A taxi!' said the exasperated officer. He took a deep breath and exhaled, shook his head in a combination of disbelief and disappointment, looked up above his glasses, and addressing Ezra directly said, 'You don't understand, we are a police force, we are not a mob. You came here in a police car and you'll go back in a police car.'

A few minutes later there was a knock on the door. A soldier entered, stamping his right foot hard on the stone floor, and saluted with his right arm, a proper military salute: 'Sir, a car is ready outside, Sir.'

Then, something remarkable happened that Ezra would never forget; the constable who slapped him so hard earlier and who had beaten the Zionist, the ever-so-happy-to-beat-anyone constable, came over, patted Ezra gently on the shoulder and said, '*Ta'al, ibni, ta'al*; come along, my son, come along. *Ta'al, ibni, ta'al.*'

They took Ezra to the airport. They gave him a chair to sit on, and there was a tap for water in the corner. It was July and very hot. In the morning, Ezra told a policeman who had just taken over guard duty that he hadn't had anything to eat for over twenty-four hours. The policeman immediately went out and bought him a huge pita sandwich. Ezra sank his teeth into it, and ate it without even examining what it was.

Abraham El-Fannan was out of breath when he arrived at Um-Kamal's; he couldn't get the words out.

'Um-Kamal, Um-Kamal...'

'What is it?'

Abraham had a unique way of telling a story. Bits of the story came out of his mouth in no particular order, much like an artist dismembering a mosaic he had constructed and passing it out piece by piece at random. Only when the pieces are reassembled in the correct order does it begin to make sense.

'Sitting, waiting – I don't know – woman next to me – Jewish – chatting – "I'm seeing my best friend off" – her son – sirens – don't understand…'

'Calm down. Take your time.'

'… everyone was looking – EZRA MAUDE ABRAHAM – police car – don't understand – pushed him out – what's going on – I waved – he started arguing – DIDN'T GET ON THE PLANE…'

'Who didn't?'

'Ezra… Ezra didn't get on the plane.'

'What do you mean, he didn't get on the plane?'

'He didn't. They took him away.'

'Who took him away?'

'The police – the police took him away, with another Jew, in a police car.'

And that's how Um-Kamal became aware that Ezra was arrested before he could get on the plane.

Um-Kamal quickly put whatever food there was in a pot, wrapped it with a cloth and, taking Elias who just happened to be off school that day, went to the CID headquarters, where all such detainees were taken. Elias noticed a towel hanging at the window, a red, yellow and blue towel with a picture of a parrot.

'Look, look Nana, that's Ezra's towel,' he said. 'He left it there to let us know he is inside.'

It wasn't safe for a woman to go into the police headquarters, so Um-Kamal handed the pot of food to Elias and told him to go in.

Elias walked gingerly up the five steep steps that led to a large, imposing door. The guard at the door looked down at him, took the food, but refused to say if Ezra was there. He then looked at Elias and said, 'You're a Jew,' and he slapped him on the face. Um-Kamal and her son went back home not knowing if Ezra was, in fact, in the station. When they went back the next day, the towel was not there.

'Ezra must have gone,' said Elias.

When Rosette came home, Um-Kamal was still sitting on the floor, looking at the letter in her lap.

'They should have taken it out of its envelope before sending it on,' said Rosette when she saw that the letter was still in its original envelope with Israeli stamps on it. 'This could land us in a lot of trouble, if anyone sees it.' Rosette took the letter out, tore the envelope into small pieces, threw them into a metal bucket, lit a match, and burned them. She waited till every piece turned into black ash, before throwing the ashes into a dust bin. She moved to the window, unfolded the letter, and began to read it. It was a long, three-page letter.

'What does it say? Is Ezra all right?' asked Um-Kamal.

'He is all right, he's managed to get a job and move out of the camp.' Rosette then proceeded to read the rest of the letter to her mother. Um-Kamal, her head slightly bent with her right hand on her mouth, eyes watering, listened attentively, asking her daughter to repeat a word here and a sentence there, making a subdued comment here, and a gasp there. When Rosette had finished reading the letter, Um-Kamal took it back, folded it, and held it close to her chest; she was determined not to cry, but one tear managed to escape her right eye, progressively disappearing as it slid down her cheek. It left no visible trace.

One by one, her children returned home and each time Um-Kamal asked each one to read the letter for her again. She listened quietly, attentively, as if trying to memorize each word, each phrase, each sentence.

Abu-Kamal was the last to arrive. 'You have a letter from your son,' said Um-Kamal. Abu-Kamal took the letter, looked at it, and put it on the bookshelf. He didn't read it; he couldn't trust himself to read it without crying. Later, when the rest of the family were in bed, Abu-Kamal went downstairs, unfolded the letter and, with the light from a candle, he read it. Tears of sadness and joy flowed freely down his face. Um-Kamal watched from the stairs.

11

Life at Qamber Ali

IT WAS ROSH Hashanah, the Jewish New Year, and it was quiet, eerily quiet. Normally at that time of year the house would be full of kids running about, shouting and laughing. Sisters, aunts, uncles and friends would visit with parcels of food and gifts for the children. Um-Kamal's father would make his annual visit and, being a market *sarraf almal*, a rudimentary street money-trader, he would hand each of the young siblings a crisp new quarter of a dinar, which Um-Kamal would confiscate the minute he was out of the door. But they had all gone, not a single relative remaining. All of them, as well as her friends, had signed up to *al-taskeet* and had gone to Israel, never to be heard from again.

A heightened sense of loneliness, abandonment, and sadness descended on Um-Kamal. She suddenly realized how empty her home had become. Her eldest daughter, now married, had been posted to Al-Diwaniyah, 100 miles south of Baghdad. Her eldest son was away in Aqrah, 300 miles to the north, Ezra had left for Israel, and Sasson was in prison. Qamber Ali used to have a thriving and vibrant Jewish community. Today, 24/143, Qamber Ali is the only Jewish house in the district.

Only the four young siblings who were still at school remained in the family home. She was worried they were growing up without knowing any of their relatives: grandparents, aunts, uncles, nieces, nephews. They did not play in the street; partly because the street was just a wide alleyway, with an open narrow channel in the middle that carried rain water and whatever waste the residents chose to throw out; but mainly because of the risk that playing in the street posed. Although the neighbours were friendly and supportive, anyone – a passer-by, a disgruntled Palestinian refugee – could turn on them. They did not mix with Muslim children. Their only friends were from Frank Iny, the one remaining Jewish school, and they lived some distance away in the more prosperous part of Baghdad.

The children readily adapted to the new life, making their own amusement and games. The two youngest spent their time rolling an inflated inner tube of a car tyre, and guiding it with a stick round and round the roof area, or focusing sun rays into a sharp point to burn a hole in a sheet of paper with a magnifying glass, invariably burning the back of their hands in the process. They imitated the sword fights they had seen on the screen on the rare occasions they visited a cinema, using metal skewers for swords. On one occasion this resulted in Sa'id, getting carried away with Errol Flynn's role as Captain Fabian, stabbing his younger brother inside the mouth.

Elias, being the eldest of the younger siblings, and having some knowledge of physics, constructed various contraptions, including a communication apparatus using two tin cans and a string, connecting to a projector using another tin can, an electric bulb and a magnifying glass. The younger ones watched him as he made two square holes in two cards and, using glue, secured the lens against one hole and a transparency which they found in a wooden box against the other. Then he pierced four wires through each corner of the cards, and placed them in front of the open end of the can. When the curtains were drawn and the light bulb placed inside the can was turned on, light was projected onto the wall, and a semblance of a picture was discerned. With their mouths open in astonishment, Farouk, Sa'id and Layla watched as Elias moved the lens slowly away from the lamp, whereupon a clear black and white picture began to be visible on the wall; an upside-down picture of a boy, about their age, sitting at a desk, pen in hand, writing. Elias, to the consternation of his younger siblings, turned the electric bulb off. He turned the transparency-holding card upside down, and turned the light on again to reveal an upright child-at-desk picture. Their eyes were transfixed by the picture on the fading brown wall, when it began to warp as the heat from the bulb began to singe the transparency.

'What is that smell?' Um-Kamal shouted from the bottom of the stairs.

'Nothing, nothing,' the children shouted back. The celluloid continued to burn. Elias quickly turned the bulb off, so the scorching stopped, and a fire was averted.

They came upon a manually operated 8mm cine projector and a canister containing 8mm cine films. There was one of the Yalta meeting between Churchill, Roosevelt and Stalin, which would have instantly landed anyone in prison if found in their possession. It was one of the many things their relatives left with Um-Kamal when they immigrated to the newly created state of Israel.

They discovered that wiping an 8mm cellulose nitrate cine film with a wet cloth removed the ink, leaving the frames clean, on which subjects could be drawn using a simple pen. Layla, being a girl with an artistic inclination, was chosen to draw a man riding a rocket. She drew an arrow for the rocket, a line for the body, a dot for the head, and two short lines for the arms of a man sitting on the arrow. By repeating the drawing on successive frames, with a circle appearing at the edge that became larger with each frame, they had a film of an erratically shaking rocket carrying a man to the moon. When the rocket reached the moon, the man leant over to look at the Earth, slipped and fell over the edge, all the way back to Earth; an ending that generated much laughter when played back on the cine projector after dinner.

Um-Kamal looked at the clock on the shelf. It had been two hours since Abu-Kamal had taken the children to Al-Sa'dun Park, the only park in Baghdad. They didn't usually venture out, but it was Rosh Hashanah, and her husband wanted to give the children a treat. She began to feel twinges of worry in her stomach. Something must have happened to them, she thought. No matter how much she reasoned with herself that the journey to the park and back alone took two hours, she couldn't stop worrying. Gradually, she entered the make-yourself-mad-with-worry-for-no-rational-reason state, a condition that afflicted most parents, but especially mothers in that part of the world: an escalating, self-sustaining state of foreboding. The level of concern exhibited was viewed as a measure of love and affection; the greater the apprehension, the greater the love. It was a way of life, a condition of existence for Jewish families.

She pushed the door open and looked out. There was no sign of them. She paced up and down. She stood still, placing her palms flat on her cheeks, a traditional gesture of fear and apprehension. She alternated between looking out of the door and pacing up and down the courtyard, until the door was pushed open and the children ran in, pushing and shoving, joking and laughing, followed by Abu-Kamal who, upon seeing his wife's drained face, the silent reproach mixed with a forced smile, immediately knew he was in for a serious rebuke later.

12

1953 – Al-Salman desert, southern Iraq

IT WAS ON the first leg of the journey; they were approaching the only scheduled stop, an oasis. It was hot and dry, but Um-Kamal refused to loosen her abaya for fear that the parcel she was carrying would be discovered. The package was heavy. It contained urgent documents that the Communist Party could only entrust her with. She had heard of several women who had been caught attempting to smuggle things into prison, and of the harsh prison sentences they then received. But that didn't deter her; she was doing it for her son. She thought that was the least she could do for him. She began to perspire heavily, gasped for air, and felt delirious and faint, but she continued to hold the parcel tightly to her chest and she drifted into a stupor.

For the nine or ten young boys who accompanied their mothers on the journey, the stop at the oasis well was the highlight of the trip – not just to leap out into the desert sand, and chase and kick each other, but as much to run to the well and be the first to get to the water pipe. This was a race in which Farouk was able to participate, because his mother was asleep and could not stop him from leaving the coach as she would have done. So, unlike his more timid brother, Sa'id, who would not take advantage of the situation, he leapt up and joined the scramble out of the coach to run the 100-metre or so distance to the water hole. Being small and nimble, he easily outpaced everyone and, just before he could claim the prize of being the first to taste the water pouring out of the lead pipe that bent over the water's edge, he looked back and saw what to him was the huge bulk of an older well-built boy, still accelerating well past the point where he should have slowed down if he was to avoid going over the edge by pure momentum. He would have done, had Farouk not been in the way and, in the manner of a fast-moving billiard ball coming into contact with a stationary one, and transferring all of its kinetic energy to it, Farouk was forcefully propelled forward and into the well, which, being just after the rainy season, had a high water level, just a few inches below ground level.

Everything went quiet as he sank into the water slowly, going down for what seemed eternity, and, having not been taught to swim, his efforts at lifting himself up only helped to pull him further down. He was drowning, unable to breath and he began to swallow water. His downward movement began to slow as the force of the fall began to fade. Then the natural buoyancy of his body began to take over. He began to float up, slowly but surely. He could see against the bright sun faces looking back at him, urging him to do this or that. He swallowed more water, his head popping up at one time over the water surface, which allowed him to take in some air. Then under the water again, so that he could only swallow water, some of which went the wrong way, into his lungs. He tried to expel the water, but couldn't. He moved his arms aimlessly and furiously, he grabbed the edge of the well with his little hand, in a fruitless attempt to lift himself, only to end up with a fistful of mud and no purchase at all. He tried again with the other hand, with the same result.

Farouk began to lose the will to fight when, suddenly, a young woman who had the presence of mind to move to the front of the agitated crowd that gathered around the well stretched out her arm, and when his head next popped out, she pushed it down with her open palm, in what seemed to be an effort to end his misery. When she lifted her hand out of the water, she held a clump of Farouk's hair and pulled a coughing, wheezing Farouk up and out over the side of the well. He was alive. Farouk sneezed, heaved, and vomited. His tummy was rumbling and he had a headache. There was no doctor or nurse present, but there was a rabbi.

The rabbi volunteered to say a prayer to dispel any demons and alleviate the pain. He took a tallit shawl out of a brown cloth bag and spread it over his shoulders, then a fading yellow yarmulke which he placed on his head. Next, he pulled out a well-thumbed, leather-backed book and held it in his left hand. He placed the palm of his right hand over Farouk's head, looked out into space, and recited a few verses in Hebrew, which no one seemed to understand. When that was done, he put everything back into the cloth case and fastened it tightly.

Everyone looked expectantly at Farouk. He was bombarded with: 'Do you feel better?' 'Has the pain gone?' 'Do you still feel sick?' With anxiously hopeful faces staring at him, he couldn't disappoint, so he said, 'Yes, much better,' if only so he could be left alone.

Um-Kamal, sensing the commotion, began to stir. To break the news gently, the nearest woman to her whispered, 'Don't worry, Farouk is all right' – a euphemism, if ever there was one, for something dreadful that had happened. Um-Kamal screamed, looked for her son, grabbed him, went pale, and fainted again. When she came to, she scolded Sa'id for not looking out for his younger brother.

* * *

FIFTY YEARS ON, after telling the story for the umpteenth time to various people, Farouk was asked if he would have liked to meet the woman who pulled him out of the well. He had never thought of it before, but he suddenly felt an urge to do so. 'Yes, I suppose I would. I never thought about it before. Yes, I would.'

And so, he went to Ramat Gan, the place where Iraqi Jews who migrated to Israel tended to settle. He found out that the woman's name was Munira, and on the day of the incident she had been visiting her twenty-one-year-old son who was serving a three-year sentence; six months before he was to be released, after completing his sentence, he had taken part in a hunger strike to force the government to move prisoners out of Nigret al-Salman and close the infamous prison. He had fallen ill and, refusing to break the strike, died. Soon after, Munira immigrated to Israel with her husband. She passed away, aged fifty-four, they say, of a broken heart. She had frequently lamented, 'They took away my only child.' Farouk, seeking some contact, went to Nahalat Yitzhak cemetery in Tel Aviv, where she was buried in a nondescript, simple plot with a 3-foot headstone inscribed with some words and dates in Hebrew.

There was a commotion at a nearby grave, where an orthodox ritual was being conducted for relatives of a dead man by a group of bearded men in black attire and black hats with ringlets hanging down both sides of their faces. They were chanting verses from a holy book they held in their hands, in a robotic, monotonous manner, showing not a vestige of emotion, and giving the impression of wishing to reach the end of the job at hand as fast as possible. They had no idea who the entombed person was, creating a hollowness and no atmosphere for any sort of quiet contemplation. The arrogance that characterizes religious zealots prevented any recognition of the intrusion they caused in other people's lives and, if the souls of the dead were aware of the living, as their faith dictates, then these souls would be howling in distress and anger, as would any living ones. After more than half an hour of what to Farouk seemed to be inexplicable and unnecessary chaos, with stones being placed on the cairn by all those present, even those who were paid to join the group to make up the minyan, the required quorum of ten men, left.

At last, Farouk was able to stand there, in contemplation. The warm sun was beginning to slide towards the horizon; all was peaceful, except for the sweet song of the common myna bird calling her mate. As he stood there, a shiver crept slowly down his back, gradually enveloping his entire being. His eyes began to well up. He asked his wife, Valerie, who had accompanied him on his journey, for a paper and pen and, leaning on his wife's back, he wrote, 'Here lies a woman, a brave woman, like so many, a product of the 3,000 years of the history of Jews in Iraq.' He took two steps forward, placed the note under a stone at the foot of the headstone, stepped back, and walked away quickly, as the tears started to roll down his face.

13

A few months later

'WHAT DO YOU mean, depressed?' exclaimed Um-Kamal. 'I've never heard anything like it. What is there to be depressed about?'

They were in Aqrah, a year into Kamal's posting. The younger children had gone to sleep in the open front yard of the clinic. Mother and son were having one of their conversations that went on late into the night, with Kamal offloading his fears for the future, his feelings of loneliness, and his deep anxieties onto his mother. He'd had hopes of working in a leading hospital at the frontier of medicine, developing new medical treatments. He wanted to get married, have a family, something that was increasingly unachievable given the few Jewish families left in Iraq. His future lay abroad, but that too was blocked.

He was trapped.

He told his mother of his recurring dream: lost, unable to find his way back home, where she was waiting for him. His psychiatrist friend from the medical school, a Jewish graduate who was posted to the border town of Al-Amadiya, north of Aqrah, said his depression was caused by his 'exile' into the remote regions of Kurdistan. 'You ought to get out of there as soon as you can,' he had written.

Kamal was on the verge of a breakdown.

'What is there to be depressed about?' Um-Kamal repeated. 'You have a good job, you're well respected and popular, everyone likes you. They come to see you from all over the place, they walk for hours to come here. Your surgery is full and you are making money.'

Kamal looked into space, but did not respond.

Um-Kamal couldn't stop herself from saying out loud what she was thinking. 'It is not as if you are in a prison,' and she immediately regretted saying it.

'But it is very much like a prison,' said Kamal.

'You are free to come and go,' said Um-Kamal. 'This is not a prison.'

'It may not be a prison, but I'm imprisoned, all the same.'

Um-Kamal was furious. She wanted to say, 'You should go and see Nigret al-Salman; *that's* a prison.' But this time she was able to keep her thoughts to herself.

'This is not a prison,' she repeated instead, 'and nobody is keeping you a prisoner.'

'Imagine,' reflected Kamal, 'someone is offered 10 dinars if he was prepared to spend one day, twenty-four hours, alone in a room with all his food and comforts catered for, 20 dinars if he stays for a subsequent day, and 40 for a third, and so on, on an exponential scale. Will he ever leave?'

Um-Kamal looked puzzled.

'No matter how much money he accumulates, the temptation is to stay one more day, to double his money,' Kamal continued. 'He'll say to himself, "Just one more day and I'll quit. What possible harm can that do?" And even when he had made a million dinars, he'll still be tempted to spend one more day to make it 2 million, and so it goes on. He'll never leave. There'll be no need for bars on the window or padlocks on the door. There'll be no need for a jailer; he is his own jailer. Baba always said, "Work now, play later." This is what he instilled in us from a very young age: work hard today, and you'll get your rewards tomorrow.' Kamal paused, and then added, 'And there is always a tomorrow.'

He was in a fragile state. Um-Kamal had never seen him like that before.

'Stop this, stop it, right now. There are people who live in squalor, can't afford a roof over their heads, or food for their children. They are not depressed. They can't afford to be depressed. They just get on with it. Think how fortunate you are,' she said. 'You could be in prison like your brother, a real prison.'

'In some ways, I wish I was.'

'What nonsense is this?' said Um-Kamal.

'In a sense, we are both in a prison.'

'Rubbish,' said his mother. 'Do you know what Nigret al-Salman is like?'

'Different prisons, but prisons, nonetheless.'

'You must stop talking like this. It doesn't do you any good. It'll only depress you.'

'I'm talking like this because I am depressed,' said Kamal quietly.

There was a pause.

'Every morning, when I wake up, I have this feeling of guilt, it overwhelms me,' Kamal said.

'Guilt?'

'I feel weak, like I have a hole in my stomach. I feel guilty.'

'Guilty? For God's sake! Guilty for what?'

'I don't know,' he said. 'I can't put my finger on it.'

'What do you mean, you don't know? You must know.'

'Difficult to say. It is as if I somehow have failed in my responsibility.'

'First, you feel guilty. Now, you're responsible. Stop tormenting yourself. Responsible! Responsible for what?'

'Responsible for what happened to Sasson.'

'*Ibni*, my son. Kamal, *ibni*. You're not responsible. The government is responsible, Nuri Al-Said is responsible, the King, his uncle, the British, they are all responsible. They are the ones who put Sasson in prison, not you. Consider yourself lucky not to have ended up there as well.'

'But I do, I do. I do consider myself lucky, very lucky. But that doesn't make it better. In fact, it makes it worse.'

Abu-Rahman walked into the kitchen area dangling a chicken by its legs. Um-Kamal was preparing to start cooking Kamal's favourite meal, *dijaj wa'erz*, chicken stew on a bed of orange chicken-flavoured rice.

'Here it is,' said Abu-Rahman. 'The healthiest, best-looking chicken in the market.'

The hen bent its neck 180 degrees, clucked a few times, and made a futile attempt at escaping Abu-Rahman's tight grip. It twisted its body and flapped its wings, but, apart from losing a few feathers that floated in the air before settling on the ground, the bird continued dangling hopelessly in space.

'I'll kill it and pluck it for you Um-Kamal?' suggested Abu-Rahman.

'No! You can't. It won't be kosher.'

'But there aren't any Jewish rabbis in Aqrah. They have all gone. You have to go to Mosul for one of them.'

'Not rabbis; *shochets*.'

'Right, *shochets*. There aren't any here.'

'*El-Duktor* can do it.'

'*El-Duktor!* But he is not a *sho*…'

'No, no, he isn't. In emergency situations where a *shochet* is not available, we are allowed to eat the meat of an animal, provided it is killed by one of us. If *el-Duktor* kills the chicken, it'll be kosher.'

She turned to her son and said, 'Kamal, *ibni*, take it to the backyard and slaughter it for me, will you?'

'The chicken? No. Let Abu-Rahman do it.'

'It won't be kosher. You have to do it.'

Kamal gestured to Abu-Rahman to take the struggling bird to the backyard.

To the amusement of Abu-Rahman, Kamal took the chicken and held it in his arms in the manner of someone holding a pet, more likely to kiss it than kill it.

Kamal handed the chicken back to Abu-Rahman and said, 'Here, you do it, but don't tell Um-Kamal.'

Abu-Rahman wasted no time. In a single twist, he broke the poor creature's neck, and with another swift circular twist he separated it from its body. The chicken struggled, slipped out of his grasp and dropped to the floor. It immediately stood on its legs and, with blood streaming out of its neck, started to run in a circle, unaware that it had left its head behind. It did a complete lap of the small backyard, and then collapsed, not far from its head. Its body twitched one last time, its head opened and closed its eyelids, and the chicken died.

'Abu-Rahman is plucking the chicken,' Kamal told his mother, when he went back to the kitchen area.

'Did you?' asked Um-Kamal.

'Did I what?'

'Did you slaughter the hen?'

'Yes, of course.'

Um-Kamal kept her suspicions to herself.

Decamping to Aqrah became an annual summer event. It was a lifeline for Kamal.

For the younger children, going to Aqrah was an escape from the exhausting heat of the capital, something that only the very rich could afford, certainly not something those who lived in Qamber Ali would have ever dreamed of. It was also a great adventure.

They took the famous steam train to Mosul, and from there a taxi across high mountains and deep valleys to Aqrah where, being *el-Duktor*'s siblings, they were treated as VIPs by the local population. It was a transformative experience for the young children. The landscape, the outdoors, the mountains, the valleys, the fast-flowing streams and tributaries, the freezing cold springs spouting out of hard rocks, and the hanging fruit. The ragged untouched terrain couldn't be more different from the inner-city slums of Qamber Ali.

They couldn't wait to explore their new surroundings. So, when Kamal decided to resume public immunization by going to Shanik, a village in the foothills of the Sinjar mountains, north-west of Aqrah, the boys were eager to join him. There was no question of their sister going. It was not an acceptable thing for a girl to do.

'*Duktor*, we don't go to remote mountain villages,' said Abu-Rahman, when Kamal asked him to make arrangements for the trip. 'There are no roads, only a mountain trail, and you'll have to stay overnight. You don't have to go. I can complete the necessary forms, get the elders to say the doctor had been there, and all you have to do is sign and send them to Mosul, no questions asked.' With a triumphant tone he added, 'If you immunize everyone, no one will get sick, and where does that leave you? You'll have no patients.'

Three mules stood in a row, their tails swaying one way and then the other, scattering the flies that settled on their backs and hips, quivering their skin in patches where a fly or two decided to land. They sniffled, snuffled, and puffed to dislodge others that found their eyes and wet noses irresistible, as they waited patiently outside the back entrance to the clinic. Abu-Rahman and the storekeeper-cum-pharmacist, Samir, brought out two heavy boxes, lifted one and dumped it on one of the mules, which had long ears and no saddle. With Samir's steadying hand, the box was balanced precariously on the animal's back, as Abu-Rahman lifted the second box and pushed it against the first, carefully dislodging it to make space for both boxes to settle on each side of the beast's back. The only protection from the rough surface of the boxes was a black rug that was fraying in several places. The two boxes were held in place by a rope that the two men fastened around the mule's bulk and tied with a large knot. The boxes secured, a blanket was thrown over them, together with several other smaller items that may have been needed for the journey. The blanket was then folded over the bulky luggage and the four corners tied under the mule's belly to keep them secure. Throughout all of this, the mule hardly twitched a muscle, remaining steady on its slender legs with its hooves stuck to the ground, as if with glue. A true beast of burden.

With the help of Abu-Rahman, Kamal and the three boys climbed onto the saddles of two mules, Kamal and Farouk onto the largest, the black mule with a white nose. Elias and Sa'id were on the light-brown mule with grey underside. Samir needed no help as he stepped on the stirrup with his left foot and swiftly lifted his right leg over before settling on the saddle of the smallest of the mules.

'Khalif will accompany you,' said Abu-Rahman. 'He is waiting for you down the valley.' With that, he let out a short burst of sibilant sounds and struck the white-nosed mule with a stick. The mule started to walk slowly at a steady pace. The light-brown mule, with

Elias and Sa'id on its back, waited till the white-nosed mule was one or two lengths ahead, and followed it in the same manner. It needed no prompting. The other two followed, making a small convoy.

The mules navigated the narrow stony path down to the valley with exceptional dexterity and competence. It was early in the morning and the valley was still under the shadow of the mountain. Khalif, mounted on a dishevelled mule, was waiting for them at the bottom of the valley.

At first, the trail to Shanik was rough, but relatively wide and level; the boys even attempted a race, digging their heels into the mule's belly to get the animal to gallop, trot, or just move faster than the monotonous steady click-clack of their hooves on the rough ground, but without any success. The track became narrower as they started to go up the side of the mountain, until it almost disappeared. However, the mules continued their steady pace, picking their footholds with startling confidence. At certain places, the boys could see no path at all, just rocks, trees and green vegetation. The mules carried on, unperturbed, placing their hooves on the smallest of ledges and managing to balance, not only their bulky bodies, but also the loads they had to carry, made difficult as their loads swayed in the opposite direction to the movement of the mules.

In places, the mountain side was so steep, Elias and Sa'id were afraid to look down. Suddenly, their mule stopped and would not move. They tried to urge it on, digging their heels into its belly, making the usual sibilant sounds, but it stubbornly refused to budge. Khalif came over and moved the beast back a couple of paces, saying that the mule had veered about a foot from the trail, realized what it had done and stopped. 'What a smart mule!' thought Sa'id. 'Talk about developing respect for animals!'

The boys held the reins tightly, Farouk grabbing the mule's neck at one time to avoid falling off. Several times they had to hunch down to avoid low-hanging branches and, at one point, Sa'id had to cling to a branch to prevent himself falling off.

When they got within sight of the village, they passed construction workers building a bridge across a ravine with a fast-flowing stream at the bottom. Elias was very impressed as he looked on. This was probably the moment when he decided he would be a civil engineer, building bridges. Eventually, he did build bridges, but in Canada, not Iraq.

The village elders were waiting when the small convoy arrived at Shanik. Precisely how they knew the doctor was coming remained a mystery for Kamal and the boys.

'We've been waiting for you *Duktor*,' said the tribal chief. He had a magnificent moustache, complemented by equally magnificent head gear, with baggy, brown-red trousers and a glittering golden threaded waistcoat.

'This is the first time we have been honoured with a visit by a doctor since his majesty came to the throne. So good to have you, come, come.' He gestured to one of the attendees, who was standing nearby, to help Kamal and the boys down from the mules. A crowd of young men, all in traditional Kurdish gear, some with rifles slung over their shoulders, gathered around.

'Move, move, let *el-Duktor* through,' shouted one the chief's minions.

It was early evening and the party was taken to the considerable residence of the tribal chief, where they stayed the night sleeping in the back garden under the stars.

In the morning, while Kamal, with the assistance of Samir, was immunizing and generally dealing with health problems of the local population, the boys were shown the chief's estate. A short, stocky man in a colourful Kurdish costume, with a rifle slung over his shoulder, took them around. They walked through rows of white-flesh peach trees, pear trees, orchards, long white grapes, and pomegranates. The three children picked fruit from low-hanging branches, cooled them in the crystal clear water of a fast-flowing stream, took big bites, and spat away the pips and seeds as they went along.

At the end of the estate, where the cultivated land came to an end, they came to a man-made circular pond supplied with fresh running water from a small stream that ran down the mountain. A rudimentary dam made of logs and stones directed the clear fresh water to the pond. The pond was emptied once a year, and it so happened that the pond was filling up when they arrived that day; it was still shallow, with the water just above waist high. The boys started to wade in, sloshing and splashing, hanging from an overhanging branch of an oak tree, and letting go to plunge into the water.

At the edge of the pool, hidden in the green shrubs, was a tree-frog, its light green colour providing a perfect camouflage. It croaked. Farouk approached the frog cautiously through the shallow water. The frog straightened its hind legs and, with a mighty jump, propelled itself into the middle of the pond. It clutched its front feet together, stretched its two front legs beyond its head, and pushed them back through the water. At the same time, it pulled its back legs towards the front, and pushed them back through the water, in perfect harmony with the movement of its front legs. It repeated this manoeuvre several times, as it swam majestically and effortlessly to the other side of the pond, where it crouched. Farouk approached the frog again. The frog jumped into the water and swam to the other side of the pond. 'So this is how you swim,' thought Farouk. He pushed himself away from the edge of the pond, and attempted to swim back, imitating the movements of the frog. He repeated this several times and gradually he started to float, with each repetition moving further and further away from the edge. When the pond was halfway full and his legs could not touch the bottom, Farouk swam back to the edge unaided. He looked around, but the frog was gone.

14

2003 – Sasson, Haifa

'IT WENT ON for two or three weeks. I don't really remember,' said Sasson.

This was December 2003. Farouk and Sasson were sitting in Sasson's sixth-floor apartment in Haifa, overlooking several other high-rise blocks that were built not that long ago. The windows were closed and the sun was casting long, pale shadows inside.

'No one outside the prison knew... we wanted people to know... one prisoner had a very loud voice: "*Today is the eighth day since food was stopped and water cut off; we are your sons; the sons of the noble people of Iraq, we are your brothers.*"

'He shouted like a town crier. The prison was in the middle of the city. The police tried to drown his voice by banging on pots and pans and anything else they had. It was surreal.' Sasson stopped, and reflecting said, 'You know, I never talked about this before.'

'You've never talked about this before? Wait, wait,' said Farouk, 'I have to record this!' Farouk got out his Dictaphone.

* * *

What Sasson found difficult to remember was the Kut prison siege in which communist prisoners were denied food and water and prevented from exercising in the yard. It lasted two weeks, and ended in a massacre. Every morning, the Governor, a short, heavily uniformed man, stood behind a large sandy-coloured megaphone which concealed all of his head and most of his upper body, commanding the 150 prisoners to: 'Stop your mutiny! Stop your disobedience.' And every morning, the prisoners shouted back, 'No, never!'

It was 1953. Sasson was twenty. This was his third year in prison.

* * *

'THEY IDENTIFIED FOUR or five to be shot, killed. You know Heskel? Yes, Heskel Kojaman; he was one of them.'

'Why Heskel? Was he part of the prison leadership?'

'No, he wasn't. He would have made some criticism of the Communist Party's tactics which did not go down well with the leadership outside. He was thoughtful and outspoken, well read, a true intellectual. If you wanted to know anything, you asked Heskel. He was the nearest thing to Google we had.'

* * *

The authorities decided to take political prisoners back to the notorious Nigret al-Salman prison in the middle of the desert, six months after the government was forced to move all prisoners out of there, following a hunger strike by the prisoners. Not all of them were going to be moved, only the Jews. All of the prisoners refused. Food supplies were stopped and water was withdrawn. The only way to get any water was to dig a well. They couldn't dig a well in the prison yard, so they dug one inside Hut 3. The water was unpleasant and salty, but it was water.

Today is the tenth day since...

Wahid Mansur was not yet eighteen. He was standing by the door of Hut 3 when a bullet from a single-shot rifle hit him in the chest. He fell back and collapsed on the floor. He was losing blood, drifting in and out of consciousness. Heskel, who was a pharmacist by trade, tried to stem the blood, but couldn't do much about the bullet, which had lodged itself deep inside, to the left of his heart. He needed hospital treatment.

Wahid opened his eyes. 'Don't let them take me,' he pleaded. 'I'd rather die.' His eyes closed and he drifted back into unconsciousness.

Sasson stuck his head out of the window. 'Mansur is wounded in the chest,' he shouted. 'He is bleeding and needs to go to hospital.'

'Bring him out,' came the reply.

'He must go to hospital, urgently.'

'Okay, bring him out.'

* * *

'WE ASKED THE authorities to take him to hospital. They told us to place him in the passage between the two doors at the prison entrance.'

* * *

The inside door opened. Sasson and Heskel carried the wounded prisoner out, through the empty prison courtyard towards the entrance under the watchful eye of prison guards stationed at the two watchtowers on each side of the entrance. The 10-foot wooden door swung on its rusty iron hinges, squeaked, and slowly opened. They laid Wahid down carefully and withdrew back to their hut.

They looked out of the window and waited. The other prisoners also looked out and waited.

* * *

'BUT WAHID HAS remained there. They did not take him to hospital.'

* * *

He was never taken to hospital. He was taken to the morgue.

Today is the thirteenth day since...
Food had almost run out. They resorted to using cod liver oil from the medical supplies for frying. Sasson hadn't had anything solid to eat for twenty-four hours, and the salty water from the well made him sick. The other prisoners did not fare much better, exhausted by the heat and sapped of energy. The five-man leadership of the prisoners remained defiant. If only they could get a word to the outside world. In such situations, the fact that no one was aware of their suffering acquired a greater significance than the suffering itself. If only the masses knew what was going on. Most of the residents of Kut did not hear the daily appeal from behind the high walls of the city's prison. The increasingly anxious cries for help did not reach them, and those who did hear shut their windows.

Today is the fourteenth day since...
Mahmood was only twenty. His task was to cut out the electric supply to the newly installed floodlights that the dreaded Director of Prisons had ordered to be erected. No longer would the prisoners

be able to escape the smothering heat inside the huts by going out into the yard, not even at night. The floodlights had to go.

Today is the fifteenth day since...

Mahmood had a rudimentary knowledge of electricity which he learned from his father, who was an electrical engineer. Attempts to take sling shots at the lights succeeded only in provoking a return volley of stones from the guards permanently stationed on the two watchtowers. Mahmood's only tool was a kitchen knife. He sharpened the knife on a whetstone, crept out to the yard, and attempted to cut through the thick electric cable feeding the large tungsten bulbs. He was soon noticed by a look-out who pointed his rifle at him, so he made a quick retreat.

'There is only one other option,' Mahmood told the leadership.

He went to the electric power socket in Hut 3 and, using a small coin, carefully took out two screws and removed the dirty black Bakelite cover to reveal two gleaming brass plates that bent around to form two protruding holes. Two thick copper wires were held tight by two brass screws. The shine of the interior belied the miserable surroundings, much like a gold nugget in a murky mountain stream. The two thick copper wires, one with a red and the other with a black sleeve, looked serene and tranquil laying comfortably in their separate brass beds, with no indication of the devastating power they could unleash if they were to share one. This is precisely what Mahmood had in mind.

'We need a strong man for this.'

A large, 6-foot, 25-stone blacksmith with long hair, square shoulders, and massive hands came forward. Mahmood took off his sweaty vest and folded it several times around the handle of the 6-inch kitchen knife.

'Hold it tight and place it across the two brass prongs. Keep your face away from it and hold it there for as long as you can.'

Mahmood stepped back. The other prisoners followed his lead. Everyone stepped back, except for the blacksmith. He held the 6-inch knife in his left hand and, with his back against the wall 3 or 4 feet away from the electrical box, he tentatively moved the knife in an arc towards the exposed socket. The knife came to rest against the wall below the 240-volt brass contacts. Nothing happened. He lifted it away and tried again, with no success.

'Move it up a little,' shouted Mahmood.

On the third try, the knife touched the terminal holding the black-sleeved copper wire, but nothing happened.

'Lay the knife flat, you must touch both–'

Sparks flew, the knife went crimson red, and the handle became red hot. The blacksmith was thrown 3 feet into the air, landing on his back, shaking and convulsing. The smell of burnt rubber, burnt cloth, and burnt flesh filled the air. The floodlights flickered, before an explosion-like bang emanating from the prison's head office shook the building. The powerful lamps that brought daylight to the prison yard at night went off, to the delight of the prisoners, but so did every other light in the prison. The two prison wings, the prison office, and the guards' sleeping quarters were in complete darkness. Everything went black, and an eerie atmosphere prevailed. For a while, everyone – the prisoners, the officers, the guards and the prison police – was stunned into silence.

Sasson and other prisoners came to the aid of the blacksmith, who continued to shake uncontrollably. Heskel laid him on his right-hand side, and kept him away from causing himself any more harm. He slowly recovered.

In the criminal wing of the prison complex, the prisoners perceived the sudden turning off of the lights as a threat, and started smashing tables and chairs, banging on doors, screaming and shouting. The prison officers, disorientated and confused, shouted random orders. The guards and prison police bumped into things, and into each other, as they tried to obey the contradictory orders.

There was mayhem all around, except inside Huts 1, 2 and 3, the political wing of the prison complex. They were quiet and calm.

The prisoners sat on the floor... waiting... waiting for what exactly? No one knew.

The night was warm. It was another tropical night, the half-moon managing to provide the flimsiest of light, and the prisoners felt safe to venture out. They streamed out from all three huts to breathe the fresh night air.

They walked out, some spreading their arms as if to embrace the heavens above, whilst others embraced each other. They didn't talk, they didn't whisper, afraid to disturb the newly established tranquillity. The prison walls dissolved into the surrounding darkness, and there was a strange feeling of relief, a sense of freedom. Above them, a vast dome was littered with millions of shining, glittering stars. They seemed so insignificant. To the south, a shooting star scarred the dark sky and withered away. Was this an omen?

Click-clung-click: the familiar sound of a bolt-action rifle being loaded. Sasson looked up, as a thin ray of moonlight bounced off the long barrel of an old Second World War rifle. He looked at Sahib who was standing next to him. They exchanged a knowing glance and turned around to run. Click-clung-click... click-clung-click; a shot rang out. Sasson looked back to see Sahib on the ground. A bullet had hit him in the back of his head. He was dead.

* * *

'IN THE END we had to give in... they were shooting, shooting at everyone in the dark. We ran back into our quarters, but they continued to shoot through the windows. They were shooting in the dark. We laid down on the floor as bullets were flying all over the place. It was brutal.'

* * *

The firing stopped.

Ten lay dead and many injured. The leadership agreed to give in. A white sheet was waved at the window, saying that they were ready to surrender.

It wasn't until seven in the morning that the prisoners were told to leave their huts, one by one.

* * *

'THEY CALLED ON us to leave, one by one. The first name they called was mine. Seven or eight people were dead.'

* * *

Sasson looked out of Hut 3. The prison door was open, and the low morning sun was shining straight into his eyes. He couldn't see much beyond the door frame. The prison yard was empty, but guards with rifles watched over him from their watchtowers. He walked across to the open door and, before his eyes could adjust to the dim light inside, he was dragged in. Prison police stood in two lines facing each other forming an arch with sticks in their hands, much like the guard of honour formed for a military or naval wedding, except in this case it was to punish and hurt those who walked through, not to honour them.

The police were shouting, sneering and swearing. Sasson hesitated. The nearest guard pulled him forward, punched him in the stomach, whilst another punched him on the back of the head. He held his arms up to protect his face, but had to continue walking, running, taking quick strides. He stumbled, fell to the ground, was kicked, then lifted himself, and was kicked again. A rifle butt collided with his chin and he began to bleed.

* * *

'All I could think of was to get through as fast as I could... I ran... I fell down... got up and ran... they were beating me on the head, face and chest, everywhere...'

* * *

He reached the outer door. The very last prison guard threw him into a waiting flat-bed lorry, where he fell on his face and fainted.

* * *

'We were taken to the hospital in Kut. The doctors and nurses were waiting for us. The hospital was told to expect a number of dead and wounded. The next day, we were all, the Jews that is, regardless of our injuries, taken on the long journey to Nigret al-Salman prison. I was relatively better than the others, with just cuts to my face and legs – not from the bullets, but from the beatings; and bruises all over.'

Sasson stopped talking and looked into space, in deep thought. 'Funny, it seems so abnormal now, yet normal then.'

'There was that time…' he continued. 'I remember now, how did we stand it all? It seemed normal, and we were young, but how did we manage it? We were in a prison in Baqubah, a new prison built with American aid. There were five of us, one was a doctor. They put us in a room, 3 by 3 metres, for a few days. I don't remember why, probably because we had sung some revolutionary songs in the yard or shouted revolutionary slogans. Why did we do that? No one could hear us. For that, some got two extra years of imprisonment. I got eighteen months more. Once, the leadership decided to put a red flag in the yard. Who was going to see it?'

Sasson stood and looked out of the window.

'Four or five days in a room the size of a toilet, five of us, tied together. We had two cans, one for toilet and another for food. The whole time, we were tied together, handcuffed. How did we manage? We suffered... what for?'

'Do you regret what happened? Are you angry?'

'No... no. It's as if it happened to someone else, and I'm just a witness.'

'Is that why you never talked about it before?'

'Maybe... maybe.'

15

Um-Kamal smuggles a radio

IT WAS MID-MORNING when there was a tentative knock on the door.

'Who is it?' called Um-Kamal.

'Um-Sasson! It's me,' called a voice she recognized. She put her abaya around her shoulders, and opened the door.

'What is it with the keffiyeh?' asked Um-Kamal, when Mohamed Saleh stepped inside.

'I think it suits me, don't you?'

'No! I don't.' She paused. 'You haven't visited me for a while.'

'I was in prison; I've just got out,' he said.

'Released or escaped?'

'What do you think?'

'Hence the keffiyeh?'

'They have the brain of a chimp. Darwin need go no further than Abu Ghraib to find the missing link.'

'But the chimps are free, and your comrades are in a cage. Some missing link!'

'My father came to visit me in prison, and when it was time to leave he gave me a robe and a keffiyeh he was hiding under his dishdasha. All I had to do was walk out, and I did.'

'Did you see Sasson?'

'No, but I met comrades who did. They say he's well, doing all right, so you don't have to worry.'

'How can I stop worrying?' said Um-Kamal. 'I heard what goes on there.'

'You know the book you smuggled into Nigret al-Salman?' said Mohamed. 'The Chinese book?'

'Yes.'

'Sasson has been translating it, page by page. They are reading it in study groups. I almost wish I was there just to read it.'

'But Sasson can't read Chinese!'

'No, no. He translated it from English. It is written by Comrade Mao Tse Tung, the great communist leader of China. *On Contradiction*, that's what it's called, *On Contradiction*.'

'I thought Stalin was the great communist leader.'

'Comrade Mao is another one.'

'Why couldn't your friend, Stalin, translate it for you?'

'Comrade Stalin is too busy for this sort of thing.'

'And how long will you be out of prison this time?' asked Um-Kamal.

Mohamed ignored her question.

'You were arrested I understand,' he said.

'Oh, that. Six months ago. I was arrested with another woman.'

'Yes, Comrade Hassibah,' supplied Mohamed. 'She is a university student. She is the one who organized the demonstration for the mothers and sisters of the prisoners on hunger strike.'

'Some organization! We almost ended up in prison. What is it with you communists? It's almost as if going to prison is an accolade.'

Mohamed nodded and smiled.

'At the start, it was going well,' continued Um-Kamal. 'We gave the leaflets away to people in the street, telling them about the hunger strike and shouting a few slogans, then, all of a sudden, the police came charging in from all directions with batons and sticks, a couple with handguns shooting in the air. Everyone ran into side streets, except for Hassibah. She only wanted to make a stand, make a speech of some kind. I held her arm and dragged her off, but it was too late. A policeman clobbered Hassibah with a baton, and I got knocked down. Before we could get up and run, we were thrown into a police van. I told her to say nothing and follow exactly what I did, or else I'd say I had nothing to do with it and that she was the ringleader.'

'She says you got her off,' said Mohamed.

'We had our faces covered, so no one knew who we were.'

'It goes to show that in a revolutionary struggle, everyone and everything has a role to play,' said Mohamed, 'even the niqab, the symbol of women's subjugation, plays a role.'

'You and your revolution,' said Um-Kamal. 'They accused us of distributing communist propaganda. I said God blessed me with a daughter, who God willed to be deaf and dumb, and an only son, the apple of his father's eye, a good boy who was dying in prison. So, I joined the demonstration to petition His Majesty, King Faisal. For the King is a good man. He is merciful and he'll understand. "Wouldn't you do the same thing if it was your son?" I said to the interrogating officer. I told them we are simple people; neither I nor my daughter can read or write, so we didn't know what was in the leaflets. I said it would be a sad day if loyal subjects cannot petition their King. Hassibah took her role seriously and was so engaged that she started behaving as if she was blind, as well as deaf and dumb. I had to remind her that she could see.'

'We were put in a cell and, within five minutes, another woman was led into the cell. She immediately took off her veil and started criticizing the government and the King. She said she was beaten up by the police and dragged through the street. Your comrade was about to say something and give the game away. I interrupted and said we were not against the police, that they were doing their duty protecting us from criminals and thieves, and that we loved the King, and his uncle had done a lot for the country. The woman soon left and we never saw her again. After two hours, they let us go. Your comrade almost put her foot in it.'

'She has a lot to learn.'

'What is she doing now?'

'She's back at college,' said Mohamed. 'We are going to get married next week.'

'Married! So you want to have someone to visit you when you are in prison.'

'We are in love.'

'Love!' said Um-Kamal. 'You'll hardly see each other.'

'The problem is she is Sunni and I'm Shia. We have to keep it quiet.'

'You do ask for trouble, don't you?' said Um-Kamal.

Mohamed stood up and walked to the window.

'The hunger strike, your demonstration, achieved its purpose; they did move them out of Nigret al-Salman.' Then, reflecting, he said, 'You know, we need people like you. We need you in the Party.'

'So, you want me to go to prison as well. No, thank you.'

'It doesn't matter how many people go to prison. It's the people themselves that count. They will rise up in a revolution and free this country from foreign control.'

'There are more communists in prison than out of prison,' said Um-Kamal, 'and the way you're carrying on, every communist will be inside.'

She went to the kitchen area, poured hot water into a tea pot and waited for the tea to brew.

'I think I've been followed,' said Mohamed.

'You think you've been followed! And you came to my house!'

'There's someone watching the house,' he said, looking out of the window.

Um-Kamal walked to the door and opened it slightly. 'Oh, that's a friend of the boys, Abraham El-Fannan. People think he's crazy, just because he plays the violin and likes to listen to Western classical music. His stepfather gives him a very hard time, calling him a locust, so he spends most of his days with us. He probably got worried when he saw you come in to the house.'

She pulled her abaya over her head, and opened the door. She avoided the braying donkey carrying the weekly rubbish in two large barrels on each side of his emaciated body, spilling their contents all along the alleyway, and went to talk to El-Fannan.

When she came back, she poured the tea, handed a cup to Mohamed and said, 'But you didn't come here just to have a chat?'

'I understand you have a visiting permit.'

'Yes, next week.'

'They need a short-wave radio.'

'A radio? What the hell do they want a radio for?'

'They want to listen to Um-Kulthum... what do you think? They want to listen to Radio Moscow,' said Mohamed.

'And how are we to get a bulky radio through the prison gates with all the inspections and guards?' said Um-Kamal.

'El-Kut is not as harsh as Nigret al-Salman. Sasson said you'll find a way.'

'Ah, Sasson! Sasson! He won't be content till his mother joins him in prison. And where am I to get a radio from?'

'There is a shop,' said Mohamed, 'a hardware shop in Kut, Abu-Omar's. That's the name of the shop, Abu-Omar's. Um-Omar will be there. Say, "It's turned out nice," and she'll reply, "You never know the weather nowadays." You then ask, "Has your daughter had the baby yet?" To which she'll reply, "It's all in God's hands." And she will hand you a parcel.'

'How would I recognize her?'

'With ease, she has only one eye.'

Abu-Omar's shop was not what Um-Kamal was expecting. There were too many people serving for a small shop, and there was no sign of the one-eyed Um-Omar. Her instincts told her to run, leave immediately, but that would raise suspicions.

'What is his size?' she asked Simran, the young woman in her twenties who accompanied Um-Kamal on her mission. Simran was taken aback at both the question and the loudness of Um-Kamal's voice.

'Was it eight? Yes, it was eight, wasn't it? Definitely eight,' Um-Kamal replied to her own question in her best Muslim dialect. She turned to one of the attendants.

'Do you have a size eight pair of gloves?'

The attendant looked as puzzled as Simran and said, 'This is a hardware store. We don't sell gloves.'

'But you do, yes, you do. Ask Abu-Omar, he'll know. Gloves, size eight, for heavy work.'

'Abu-Omar is not here.'

'Oh, is he ill? I hope he is okay. Ask Um-Omar... where is she?'

'She is not here, she is looking after Abu-Omar.'

Simran suddenly realized what was going on, and, holding Um-Kamal's arm, started to pull her towards the exit.

'What, is he so sick? Send him my best wishes,' said Um-Kamal. 'Such a nice man, so helpful, and his wife. I hope he gets well soon.

Tell him I'll drop in tomorrow.' And with that, they left the shop. Um-Kamal felt her companion's arm trembling.

'You almost got us caught,' said the young woman. 'We should have left immediately.'

'Now that would've definitely got us caught–' but, before she could explain, a man with a heavy beard and moustache, who was walking a few yards behind them, came alongside and, looking straight ahead, said, 'Um-Sasson?'

Um-Kamal continued walking and did not answer.

'You never know the weather nowadays.' And with that, he walked on, muttering, 'Follow me.'

After turning left into a narrow alleyway and walking for a few minutes, the bearded man went into a house and left the door open. They followed him in.

'Close the door behind you,' beckoned a voice from inside.

They entered the room from whence the voice came. The blinds were drawn and the room was in semi-darkness. A white-eared bulbul in a wire cage spread its small wings and started to sing a complicated set of notes, which bulbuls are famous for, stopping only to jump from one perch to another.

The voice said, 'Never mind Farad, he gets excited every time someone comes in the house. He's our early warning system.'

Um-Kamal could discern a woman sitting on a large bamboo sofa who, upon seeing them, got up and stretched out her arms, saying, '*Ahlan, ahlan*, Um-Sasson, so nice to meet you at last. I've heard so much about you.'

Um-Kamal reciprocated with open arms, a gentle embrace with two kisses on each cheek. It was then that she noticed the missing eye.

'Um-Omar?'

'Sorry about the secrecy. They raided the shop last night. Abu-Omar was arrested, but he managed to delay them long enough for me to jump out of the first-floor window and come here. You must be exhausted. Take off your abayas; we are all family here. Come, sit down, sit down. Do you want a drink of something?'

'Yes, please. Tea would be nice,' said Simran.

'We don't really have much time,' said Um-Kamal, thinking the police could soon be raiding this place too. 'Have you got the parcel?'

'Dawood has gone to get it. You know, the bearded, young handsome man who brought you here? He is such a nice lad, so polite, he'll do anything for the Party. I told him to shave that dreadful beard and he could have any woman he wanted. He said it is a disguise. Some disguise! He's had that beard for well over two years. It would be a disguise if he shaved it off.'

Um-Kamal, remembering the secret exchange they were supposed to have had, said, 'You have a daughter?'

'Alas, no. Allah didn't bless us with a daughter. I had a son. Omar was our one and only son. They came one day, broke down the door, and arrested everyone in the house. Our neighbour, who came to borrow a cup of rice, and my brother who was visiting from Al-Diwaniyah were also arrested.' She went on, 'They took my son to the Central Police Station. He was shackled in iron chains on a bare floor, with no bedding of any kind, beaten and tortured for six days and nights.' She paused to compose herself.

'On the seventh day, he died. They gave us his body. His arms, legs, front and back, were covered with cuts and bruises. His face was swollen, his eye sockets and nose broken. Abu-Omar couldn't look. I could hardly recognize him.' She paused, holding back the tears.

'Did they torture you?' asked Um-Kamal.

'Yes. How do you think I lost my eye, and why do you think Abu-Omar walks with a stick?'

Um-Kamal and Simran moved to sit on the sofa either side of Um-Omar.

'What will you do now?' asked Um-Kamal.

'I'll stay here for a while. They will soon get bored and let Abu-Omar go, and then we'll go back to the shop,' replied Um-Omar. 'They have these waves of arrests and interrogations from time to time. It is a way of impressing Nuri Al-Said and his British masters, and pretending they are doing something. They don't want any more prisoners.'

'Abu-Aslam, up the road from us, he reared pigeons, all kinds of pigeons. His most prized pigeons were two pure white doves which he refused to sell to anyone. They put him in jail, saying that the doves were communist symbols of peace,' said Um-Kamal.

Smiling, Um-Omar said, 'And how about the guy who had a thick moustache? They picked him up in the street and took him to the police station.' Laughing, she added, 'They said it was a Stalin moustache.'

The other women joined her in muted laughter. It was a moment of amusement in the midst of adversity; a moment that punctuated the pain and suffering, and so necessary if they were to come out the other side of it with their humanity intact. It is these moments that are remembered when the suffering ends and the pain is gone. It was these stories that were remembered, that were retold, over and over again, stories that generated the laughter. It was a way of remembering the bad times, by recalling the comical episodes in between.

'My brother was picked up at the Habaniya Secondary School where he worked as a geography teacher,' said Simran. 'He put up a map of the world, which included Russia, with a few prominent cities identified like Leningrad and Stalingrad. They came into the classroom, ripped the map off the wall, beat him up and took him away. We didn't know what happened to him till we read it in the papers. He got five years. They sent him to Nigret al-Salman.'

'Abu-Omar swore he'll revenge his son's death,' said Um-Omar. 'He swore he'll eat a piece of Nuri Al-Said's flesh.'

'They do have a lot to answer for,' said Um-Kamal.

'Yes, they do; they do indeed, and they will, they will soon, very soon,' said Um-Omar.

'Allah will punish them,' said Um-Kamal.

'Allah will, indeed. But, before that, we will.'

Holding Um-Omar's hands, Simran said to her, 'We've all suffered, and you more than most, Um-Omar.'

The three women sat in silence; there was no need for words. There was a bond between them, the sort of bond that binds total strangers, women with shared adversity. There was no need for more talking. They were not downhearted, as they contemplated revenge; the greater the pain, the sweeter the revenge.

The bulbul flapped his small grey wings and gave a loud rendition of its favourite tunes. Dawood came in carrying a large parcel.

'Make way, make way, the woman is heavily pregnant,' shouted Um-Kamal, as she guided Simran, wearing a large abaya covering a pronounced protrusion in her lower belly, towards the iron-strengthened, thick wooden prison gate. With her youngest daughter, Layla, in tow, they made their way through the crowd of women who gathered outside the gate waiting to be allowed in to see their loved ones. They made way, shifting this way and that, for Simran, Um-Kamal and her fourteen-year-old daughter to go through. Um-Kamal showed Simran's visiting permit, as well as hers and her daughter's, to the two guards, one a large man with square shoulders, the other a short plump woman in the traditional abaya, and continued through the gate.

'Hold on, hold on,' shouted the square-shouldered guard. 'Not so fast.'

'The woman is pregnant; she is going to faint. She has to sit and rest,' said Um-Kamal. 'Do you want to kill her?'

'No. She must be searched. She could be carrying anything.'

'She's carrying a baby. Here, look,' and she pulled Simran's abaya around to reveal a plain grey dress stretched to its extremity, covering a large lump. There was an audible gasp from the women. Some looked at the guard and shook their heads in disgust.

'There!' Um-Kamal said to the shamed guard, who instinctively averted his gaze from Simran; and, raising her voice for everyone to hear, she followed with, 'Are you satisfied now?' She pushed Simran through the half-opened gate. Simran pulled her abaya tightly around herself with her trembling right arm and walked through. Um-Kamal waited to be searched by the embarrassed female guard. Her daughter was quickly dispensed with, and after searching the basket of bread, Iraqi salad and kebab, the fruit and vegetable bag, and a box full of towels, soap and other necessities that the prisoners were deprived of, all three walked into the prison open courtyard.

When they left, a casual observer would have confidently concluded that the pregnant woman who went into the prison three hours previously had had her baby, and for an unfathomable reason decided to leave the prison without her newborn.

16

Farhud

UM-KAMAL WAS EXHAUSTED. She sat on the courtyard's stony floor to keep herself cool, holding a delicate glass of chai in her right hand. It was a pleasant morning. The sun had not yet drowned the small courtyard with its scorching ultraviolet rays. She could hear the pigeons cooing in their cage on the roof. Soon, she'll have to start cooking.

As always, her thoughts began and ended with Sasson. It had been eight years to the day since he had been arrested. He would have been out today, had he not had his sentence lengthened by eighteen months. Sasson was her favourite; caring and considerate, and never complained. He didn't even complain about the prison conditions.

She recalled the time he had offered to teach her to read and write when he had started school.

'Nana, it's easy, what they teach me at school, I'll come home and teach you,' he'd said, but she never took the offer up.

She gently wiped a tear from the corner of her left eye. She could shed a tear or two now there was no one around.

Only the younger four of her eight children remained in the family home in Qamber Ali, the home that originally belonged to her parents who, following the bomb explosion in Masuda Shemtob synagogue, decided, like the vast majority of Jews, to put their names down for *al-taskeet* – the law allowing Jews to surrender their Iraqi nationality and fly to Israel. Initially, when the law came into force in March 1950, not many chose to sign up.

* * *

'The bombs changed all that,' said Um-Kamal, now in her eighties.

'What bombs?' asked Farouk. This was his first visit to his mother's apartment in Ramat Gan.

'The bombs that went up in two synagogues in Baghdad.'

'I heard about it,' said Farouk. 'Did they find out who did it?'

'We thought it was the Muslim Brotherhood or Palestinian refugees, certainly Muslims; but it turned out to be a couple of Zionists, would you believe? Jews bombing Jews! They brought back memories of the night of *al-Farhud*, back in 1941, before you were born.'

* * *

It was on Sunday June 1, 1941 that the short-lived, pro-Nazi regime of Rashid Ali came to an end. Um-Kamal was pregnant with Sa'id, and Layla was the baby of the family. Rashid Ali had run away, as a British column from the military base in Habaniya reached the eastern bank of the Tigris. Inexplicably, the British, with the King in tow, decided to camp there overnight, leaving Baghdad with no government and no police force. It was *al-Farhud*, the breakdown of law and order. It was an open invitation for all kinds of thugs and villains, not to mention fascist gangs that had seen their leader flee the capital, to loot, burn, maim and kill. Some tribal people, many from outside the city, on horseback, joined in.

Abu-Kamal left work and hurried back. He had just managed to avoid the mobs of Muslims in tribal gear, brandishing tribal swords, marching through the alleyways of the main market towards the poor Jewish districts of Baghdad, smashing and looting any Jewish shops whose owners were in too much of a hurry to bring down the shutters.

For someone who had served in the British army, albeit as an interpreter, and survived the famous 'siege of Kut', it was surprising how anxious and scared he was made by the slightest altercation. He entered the house in an agitated state. 'Um-Kamal, they are coming to kill us,' he shouted to his wife, who was sipping tea with Um-Karim, the Muslim landlady, a blind woman who came with her young shy daughter every Monday to collect the rent, but who, on this occasion, came a day early. When she saw Abu-Kamal, she wrapped herself tightly with the abaya that was strung over her shoulders. The children were already at home, as Jewish schools closed early.

'Abu-Kamal, calm down,' implored the blind landlady. 'No one is going to harm you.'

'They're already looting El-Takya,' he continued. 'They will be here soon. It's just a matter of time.'

'*B'dalak*, don't fret,' said Um-Kamal. 'We'll leave, go somewhere safe.'

'Too late, too late,' cried Abu-Kamal. 'I told you we should have gone to my brother's. It's too late now.'

And it was too late; the sound of bricks and stones shattering plate glass could be heard from a distance. People were screaming, running, jumping from one roof to another, others fighting back. Doors were being broken, houses looted, shops burned, people raped, and men, women and children maimed and murdered. It would only be a matter of time before they reached their house, and there was nowhere to go.

'Don't worry, we'll stay with you. We'll make sure you're all right,' said the blind landlady.

She turned in the direction of her daughter, who nodded in agreement.

The blind landlady stood up, walked to the door, and stood at the entrance.

And surely, they came; six or seven young ruffians carrying knives and assorted makeshift weapons, led by an axe-carrying man in his thirties, with black hair and unkempt moustache, brown teeth, and pronounced black eyebrows.

'*El-Yahud*, where are they, where are the Jews?' the axe-carrying hoodlum demanded.

The blind woman stood in the doorway and bravely refused to budge, her trembling daughter beside her.

'*El-Yahud* aren't here,' Um-Karim shouted back, waving her cane indiscriminately, catching one of the intruders on the nose, but mainly making alternate contact with the left and right sides of the doorway. 'Go away, there is nothing for you here.'

'You're blind, you can't see,' shouted a youth, with an elongated brown birth mark on his lower cheek. 'Clear off, old woman.'

The axe-wielding hoodlum, urged on by his fellow would-be looters and killers, and employing the traditional logic of a bully, said, 'If you have nothing to hide, why don't you let us in?'

'You're blind, so how do you know there are no Jews here?' shouted another, with a pronounced stammer.

'You should be ashamed of yourselves,' the blind woman responded. 'Bullying an old, blind woman. Allah will punish you' – and, speaking directly to the axe-wielding leader, she added, 'What will your mother think? What would she say? Have some respect. Leave us alone.'

Her cane was moving erratically, hitting the stone floor and making a sound that could be interpreted as threatening but in reality was caused by her trembling hand.

There they stood, staring at each other; the ruffian, axe in hand, with his sunken eyes wide open, transfixed by the old lady, like a deer caught in the headlights of a car, and the blind woman staring back, her eyes piercing and steady, seeing more than most sighted people could ever hope to see, sensing the sweat on her interlocutor's brow. A standoff ensued between the age-old Arab tradition of respect for women and generosity of spirit and the newly acquired animosity to the Jews who, not long ago, had been considered brothers and sisters.

Unsure of the outcome of this confrontation, the young daughter slowly retreated.

Meanwhile, the next-door neighbour, a man with the name of Abu-Ahmed who spent more time drinking and beating his wife than working, jumped the narrow gap between the flat roof of his house and that of his Jewish neighbours, and, machete in hand, started to make his way down the stairs to the courtyard.

All escape routes had now been closed.

The young daughter, sensing the imminent danger, went back into the main room where Um-Kamal's family were hiding, only to find the room empty. There was no sign of anyone, no movement, save for the small door to the cupboard-sized storage room being pulled shut from inside. They – all eight of them – were hiding in that tiny space. The landlady's daughter instinctively moved towards the storage room door and swiftly pushed it shut, turned the metal lever into its latch, and stood in front of it, in the most casual way that she could muster. The lives of those inside, and probably hers and her mother's, depended on her being calm, with an air of indifference. How eight bodies managed to squeeze into the tiny space, together with a mop, a bucket and other household goods, did not occupy much of her thought. The sound of the machete-wielding neighbour stepping down the stairs became louder and more threatening. Baby Layla, who so far had been in blissful sleep, began to stir and, opening her eyes and seeing nothing but darkness, inhaled deeply – the first step in the process of letting out a screeching cry. Rosette, holding the baby in her left arm, anticipating all of that, blindly rummaged through the various items in the storage room with her right hand and stumbled upon a sugar bowl that was only brought out on special occasions, with two lumps of sugar still inside. She grabbed them and shoved one into the baby's tiny mouth. The sweet taste pacified the little girl.

There they remained in the dark, in silence, dreading even to breathe, listening and sensing.

The standoff at the main door was broken by the blind landlady.

'*Yallah imshi*. Go, my son, go; *imshi ibni, imshi*.'

She addressed the axe-wielding hooligan in that unique mixture of disapproval and forgiveness that reminded him of the way his mother reproached him when he threw stones indiscriminately at passers-by, or stole sweets from Abu-Ja'afar's stall. The other hooligans looked confused and started to push forward, eager to get on with it, when he abruptly pushed back, looked down in embarrassment and said, '*Ummi*, don't fret, we mean you no harm. We're going.' He turned around and gestured to the others to leave.

'Let's go, there's nothing here for us.'

He left, followed by his disgruntled companions.

The blind landlady swung the door shut, only to find her cane stuck between the door and the door frame. She pulled it back, shut the door with a satisfying bang. She turned around, looked into space, and started calling on Abu-Kamal, just as the neighbour with the machete descended the stairs into the courtyard.

'Abu-Ka–'

Her daughter, sensing the danger, came out into the courtyard.

'Abu-Ahmed, what are you doing here?' she asked casually. 'And what do you think you're going to do with that machete, slit our throats?'

'I heard them, they are here, *el-Yahud*,' he said. 'Let me see.'

He walked into the main room, followed by the young daughter who was not going to let him out of her sight. The blind landlady, disorientated now, walked in the opposite direction.

'What's in there?' said the intruder, pointing to the small door.

'Just a storeroom,' replied the young girl. 'Here, do you want to look?'

She moved towards the latch and started to lift the lever when, to her relief, he replied, 'Not necessary.' He turned and left the way he came.

And that's how they spent the night of *al-Farhud* – terrified, exhausted, but forever grateful to their Muslim landlady, her daughter, and that lump of sugar.

Early in the morning, they heard the crackling of machine gun fire. The army had descended on the capital, clearing the streets of mobs and looters. Later, Karim, the blind landlady's son, an army sergeant himself, a huge guy with a mighty moustache, looking elegant in his army uniform, dropped by to see if his mother's house had been looted and, to his surprise, found his mother and sister there. He said all Jews had been asked to gather at the main police station to ensure their safety, and he was prepared to escort them there. He assured Abu-Kamal that it was safe to go out.

'Come and look.'

Abu-Kamal was too scared to go alone. His wife went with him. It was true.

All was peaceful and quiet; the shops were open, selling bread and vegetables. But there was something uncomfortable in the air, an eerie quietness, with many Muslims too ashamed to look the Jewish couple in the face.

The aftermath of the night of carnage was there to be seen as they walked the Baghdad streets and alleyways to the police station. Houses had their doors broken and windows smashed, with clear signs of looting, others were burned down. A limb protruded from under a rusty corrugated metal sheet; a swarm of flies gathered, making a loud hissing noise as they devoured the dead flesh.

They were quickly joined by other Jews walking slowly in the same direction; someone with a broken leg, aided with a makeshift crutch, several with slashed faces. Two marsh harriers and an eagle menacingly circled the clear blue sky.

The open-air cinema adjoining the police station was used as a holding post for the thousands of distraught Jews, bewildered and confused by what had just happened. They asked each other about a family member, a relative, or a friend. Tales of violent atrocities and horrific cruelties mingled with stories of heroic resistance and generosity of Muslim neighbours, and friends who protected them, some at a serious cost to themselves.

There were rumours of hundreds killed and scores of women raped.

On that day, the seeds of fear, mistrust and suspicion were sown.

They were there for three days and nights, surviving on a diet of bread, cheese and cucumber that was thrown out at random from the back of open trucks twice a day.

* * *

'ARE YOU SAYING that had it not been for these bombs, the Jews wouldn't have left Iraq?' asked Farouk.

'Some would have, but the majority wouldn't,' said Um-Kamal.

Later, sitting at a café on Herzl Street, not far from Um-Kamal's apartment, Farouk reflected that had his brother not gone to prison, he could have ended up in Israel himself, as almost all Iraqi Jews did back then.

A woman approached. 'May I sit here?' she said, pointing to an empty chair at his table. There were no free tables, and she wondered if she could share his. He said she could, and a conversation ensued, as it does in countries where people spend most of their time outdoors. It turned out that, like him, she had been born in Iraq. They spoke in Arabic, with Farouk trying his best to recall a language he had long forgotten, owing to lack of practice. They reminisced about Baghdad, where they had both spent their early childhood.

'You never forget Iraq,' she said, 'it stays with you.'

'Do you regret coming here?' Farouk asked.

'No, not regret. I just wish I hadn't had to,' she replied.

17

1957 – Qamber Ali, Baghdad

THE POLICE CAR parked at the top of the alleyway, and Sasson, handcuffed to a plain-clothed police officer, walked through the narrow path to Um-Kamal's house. The four younger children were there, dressed in their finest. Farouk wore a blue-grey jacket with a zip on the front; the first new item of clothing he'd ever had bought for him. He was very proud. Upon seeing such a luxurious looking jacket, Sasson said, 'I see we've joined the bourgeoisie now.'

There was an air of excitement mixed with trepidation. Sasson wanted to spend time in the family home, albeit for just a few short hours. Um-Kamal wanted to hold him and feel his presence. Abu-Kamal wanted to see his son, look at him. He hadn't seen him since the day he was taken away. The four young children wanted some words of wisdom from their hero. But they were shy, and they avoided eye contact. Sasson moved with ease, given the fact that he was permanently attached to the policeman. It seemed almost natural.

Um-Kamal gave Sasson a big hug. She kept feeling his skinny arms. He was thin, his face almost gaunt. She wished he could stay for a week, to feed him properly and put some flesh on his bones. Abu-Kamal looked on and said very little. For an onlooker, it would be very difficult to tell what he was thinking. He wasn't angry with his son or disappointed, he knew his son was fighting a just cause, but why do those who fight for honourable causes always have to suffer pain, and those who inflict the pain seem to get away with it. He did not believe in divine retribution, but it would have helped him if he did.

Sasson was allowed to have a shower and a change of clothing. Um-Kamal had bought him a new white shirt and a dark blue suit. When they sat at the table for the special meal of *dijaj wa'erz*, the classic Iraqi Jewish dish, Um-Kamal asked the officer to remove the handcuffs. 'It's not as if he's going to fly away,' she said. The officer was only too willing to accommodate her, for it restricted his movement as it did Sasson's. He sat contently at the table, eating and burping several times. He complimented Um-Kamal on her cooking. 'I say one thing about *el-Yahud*, you Jews can't half cook.'

Sasson asked the police officer if he could go upstairs. He wanted to look around the house for one last time before he left the country. The police officer was reluctant at first, but changed his mind when Um-Kamal handed him a large slice of an apple cake she had baked.

The children joined their brother, jostling for best position to be near him. He stretched his arms around his three brothers and sister, keeping them as close to him as possible, to make contact, a simple physical contact that forges the bond between family members – the contact that was torn away by his imprisonment.

The children wanted to talk about politics, but he wanted to know what they did at school, their hobbies, what were their ambitions, what they liked and disliked, their favourite singers and their favourite songs. Mundane things; mundane and underrated, yet they are the things that unite and bring families together. They showed him the largest of the rooms, with two windows, one above the narrow alleyway that ran by the side of the house and another overlooking the wide alleyway in front. The room had two beds pushed against opposite walls, with little space between them, and a table holding several books, two pencils and a rubber, and a chair in the opposite corner. The three young boys shared the room, Farouk and Sa'id sharing one bed and Elias occupying the other.

Then they went to the smallest of the three rooms, where Layla slept.

Sasson looked up, examining the ceiling. Standing on tiptoes, he stretched out his right arm and tried to reach it. He couldn't. He picked up Farouk, put him on his shoulders, and asked him to push against the ceiling.

Farouk looked up. Elias looked up. Layla looked up. Sa'id looked up.

They noticed a square panel that they had never noticed before, a cut-out of no more than 10 inches in length, which had been neatly sawed from one of the wooden slabs that covered the ceiling. Farouk lifted his arm and pushed against the panel, but nothing happened.

'Try harder,' urged Sasson. 'Push harder.' Farouk did, but the panel wouldn't shift. Farouk clenched his fist and punched the obstinate piece of wood. He punched it as hard as he could – the panel dislodged itself from the wood it had attached itself to, through years of dust, dirt and heat; it flew up into the cavity between the ceiling and the roof. Farouk screamed, as his knuckles were bleeding, and he twisted backwards. Sasson lost his balance and Farouk landed on the floor with a bang. The noise perturbed the police officer. 'What are you doing up there?' he shouted, with his mouth full of the last spoonful of the cake he was still devouring, spitting crumbs everywhere.

'Nothing,' came a quick reply from Sasson. 'It's just my young brother messing around.' This seemed to reassure the officer. He wiped the remnants of the cake and a small bit of apple off his mouth and chin with a handkerchief Um-Kamal passed to him to keep him happy.

Sasson lifted Farouk up again. Farouk was reluctant to push his hand into the dark space that no one was aware existed, but not wanting to disappoint his brother, he pushed his arm in, feeling with his fingers, and withdrew it sharply. There was something there.

'Bring it out,' said Sasson, in a quiet voice.

What Farouk pulled out was a book covered with thick dust. He gave it to Sasson, who brushed the dust off its cover: *A Tale of Two Cities* by Charles Dickens. He flicked through it, and a thin mist of dust flew into the air. He pulled out a folded sheet of paper, which he carefully unfolded. It had the hammer-and-sickle emblem in the top right-hand corner, with the Communist Party's iconic slogan '*For a free homeland and a happy people*' in bold lettering in the middle, and beneath that '*Members of cell no. 22 of the Qamber Ali branch of the Communist Party of Iraq*', followed by a list of a dozen or so names. The name at the top was Kamal's, code name 'Al-Saqer', the Falcon. Most of the other names were familiar to him from his years in prison. Sasson didn't look for his name. It wasn't there.

He tore the paper into small pieces, squashed them tightly into a small ball, and gave it to Elias.

'Dispose of it. Burn it as soon as I leave.'

Sasson picked up Farouk again, and told him to put the displaced cut-out back in its place. The cut-out had a flange preventing it from dropping through the square hole and, when Farouk manoeuvred it into position, it sat snugly in place, revealing very little of its secrets.

'Is this where you–' Farouk began.

'Just get rid, burn it,' interrupted Sasson. 'And get rid of the book.' With a loud voice he said, 'Now I'll show you where I used to sleep.'

Elias did burn the paper, but they did not get rid of the book. They read it in turn, and in secret.

Two days later, Um-Kamal and her husband stood waiting at the departure lounge of the Baghdad International airport. A single-engine plane was already waiting for passengers to board the aircraft for Beirut, its engines whirling and propellers turning. Five minutes before the stated departure time, Sasson, dressed in the suit Um-Kamal had bought him, with white shirt and a blue and white striped tie awkwardly knotted around his neck, was flanked by a police officer and khaki-clad constable.

'You have two minutes,' said the plain-clothes man. Um-Kamal hugged her son tightly, and pursed her lips to stop herself sobbing. She was swamped with conflicting emotions; happy for her son to be leaving prison, and sad for him to be leaving her. She just managed not to cry.

'Your father suffered a lot, you know,' whispered Um-Kamal into her son's ear. 'Apologize for the heartache you gave him.' Sasson kissed his father's hand and said sorry for the suffering he had caused him.

'*Maykhalif*, it's okay,' said Abu-Kamal, in a quiet voice. He too just managed not to cry.

The officer handed Sasson a pen, and asked him to sign on a page of what looked like a passport, then walked with him to passport control and off to the plane.

After a change of planes at Beirut, Sasson landed in Istanbul. He followed the other passengers to passport control.

'What is this?' asked a burly Turkish officer with a big moustache.

'A passport, my passport.'

'This is not a passport,' exclaimed the officer in Turkish, which Sasson, not speaking a word of Turkish, understood somehow to mean this was not a passport. The officer said a few more words in Turkish and then disappeared with the disputed passport. When he came back, he was accompanied by what appeared to be a senior officer, who had a more stylish, well-pressed uniform than his more junior colleague. He looked at Sasson, and said in perfect Arabic, 'You are a Jew, yes?'

Sasson nodded.

'I thought so. This here is not a passport; it's a *laissez-passer*, a special permit to travel and only to this airport.'

Then, reading from the passport, he added, 'Issued on January 2, 1958 by the Royal Kingdom of Iraq, issue number… *one!* This is a rarity, the very first *laissez-passer* ever issued by the Iraqi government,' and, laughing, he said, 'You *must* be very special.'

The senior officer lifted a large rubber stamp from the desk and, before landing it on the passport asked, 'How long do you intend to stay in Turkey?'

'Till I make arrangements to fly to Israel.'

'You'd better hurry up; this passport expires in a week.'

He gave the unsuspecting document a very hard bang that shook the desk.

'Where shall I go now?' asked Sasson.

'Anywhere you like – you can go anywhere you like.'

'Anywhere you like,' repeated Sasson to himself. 'Anywhere you like.' He had not heard that said for a very long while.

Out of the airport, into daylight, Sasson found freedom overwhelming. He resisted the temptation to rejoice, to throw his arms in the air to celebrate his freedom; that would legitimize imprisonment, make incarceration the norm, and freedom an exception; something to be celebrated like a holiday or a birthday. Holding his suitcase, he walked fast, for no other reason than because he could. There was a taxi rank and what looked like a bus station in the distance, which seemed the obvious place to start his new life.

Halfway towards the bus stop, a well-suited gentleman walking towards him suddenly stopped and, looking at him, said, 'Do you want Israeli nationality?'

'Yes, but how did you know who I am?'

'We have ways, we have ways,' came the reply. 'Come with me, we have a room for you.'

It was his first time in a hotel. He sat at the small desk in his room and began to write:

I open my diary and with it a new life.
After 8 years, 9 months and 23 days of imprisonment and detention, I find myself on a plane transporting me to Beirut and from then on to Istanbul,
And to... Israel, my new country.
At 5:50 I bade farewell to my father and mother at the airport.
My heart overflows with emotion towards this mother who overwhelmed me with her emotions.

Sasson was spared the degrading camp accommodation that greeted the new arrivals from the Middle East, because when he landed at Tel Aviv airport, Ezra was waiting for him.

18

July 14, 1958 – Revolution

It was a normal day. Baghdad was just waking up, when the haunting voice of Abdul Basit reciting the Quran filled the air, as Radio Baghdad began its daily broadcast at half past six in the morning. Maurice, a school friend of Farouk, who, though only fourteen, was allowed to drive the family car, came over to pick up Farouk and his brother Sa'id to go for a swim in the Tigris, which was something that they did almost daily. The roads were empty, except for two or three soldiers who were hanging around Al-Rashid roundabout, and one or two army trucks crossing King Faisal II Bridge.

'It is the army going to Jordan to help King Hussein,' explained the boatman, as he pushed the boat out into the smooth waters of the river. He leaned back and pulled on the oars; the boat drifted away from the muddy shore. When he reached the middle of the river, he lifted the oars out of their wooden oarlock and placed them neatly inside the boat. The three teenagers took off their tops and prepared to jump into the water.

They could hear the puffing of heavy vehicles to their right; they looked over to the bridge, where more military vehicles, trucks and tractors were hurrying across it. There was a distant sound of gunfire. The boatman sensed something unusual, lifted the oars back onto their oarlocks, and said, 'Sorry boys, there will be no swimming today. We're going back.'

The roads were still empty. The capital was still asleep, except for the hurried movement of army trucks and armoured carriers. Fumes filled the air, and a sandy-coloured Valentine Mk III British tank parked itself in the middle of Al-Rashid roundabout, with two soldiers sitting on its armour-plated front, casually sharing a smoke.

'Shush, shush,' said Um-Kamal, as they came through the door and into the main room. The Murphy valve radio was on, and Um-Kamal, Abu-Kamal, Layla and Elias gathered around it, listening, with astonished expressions on their faces. Booming out of the loudspeaker came:

'This is the voice of the Republic of Iraq. First communiqué from the Military Revolutionary Council of the Republic of Iraq...'

The voice was calm and reassuring, with a hint of contained excitement. They were stunned. Baghdad known, at the time, as the Bastille of the Middle East, was liberated on Bastille Day. The symbolism didn't escape the announcer, who dubbed the overthrown kingdom the *Ancien Régime*.

The voice from the radio faded out, as the radio waves bounced off the walls of the main room. Elias attempted to re-tune the radio, turning the brown plastic knob on the side of the glass dial a degree or two clockwise; the needle moved to the right, the radio spluttered and hissed, so he turned the knob the other way, and the needle moved to the left, and again the radio spluttered and hissed. He returned the dial back to its original position. Farouk inadvertently touched the thin tin wire that extended up the wall towards the window. Martial music blurted out. Farouk instinctively pulled his hand away, and the music vanished, so he put his hand back, and the loud martial music returned. It was imminently, calmly, interrupted:

'This is the voice of the Republic of Iraq; the voice of the long-suffering Iraqi people. The Hashemite monarchy is overthrown by the people's armed forces and a People's Revolutionary Council has been set up. This is the second communiqué of the Military Revolutionary Council...'

So, finally it had happened.

It was like someone had released the lid of a pressure cooker. The whole of the population of Baghdad was out, or so it seemed. The streets were swarming with people celebrating the overthrow of the government. They sang, they danced, and they laughed; soldiers were hugged and kissed; women gave them tea and biscuits and kids handed them flowers.

King Faisal II Bridge was completely blocked with Baghdadis walking towards the King's residence, and among them were Sa'id and Farouk, who, against their mother's wishes, were determined not to miss out on this momentous day. As they slowly moved along the bridge, Sa'id wondered how the government had managed to keep this mass opposition under control. The image of his brother, Sasson, flashed in front of him, and he wished he was here to enjoy it.

Upon reaching the other side of the bridge, Farouk could see the white walls of the Royal Palace, but could not make out what everyone was pointing at. Suddenly, Sa'id held him by the shoulders and abruptly turned him around, away from the palace.

'You don't want to see that,' he said. The sight that Sa'id was determined that his younger brother should not lay eyes on was the corpses of the 23-year-old King and his ageing uncle, Abdullah, dangling over the palace wall. The revolutionary armed forces were not taking any chances.

'Best go to Rosette's,' said Um-Kamal. 'There is safety in numbers.'

The night of July 14 was tense. Um-Kamal's family watched from the balcony of her daughter's apartment overlooking the Al-Karkh intersection, as army cars, jeeps and troop carriers drove up and down at speed. The streets were empty, because the curfew was being fully observed.

There was the sound of a big explosion. 'Look,' said Farouk, pointing to the smoke rising on the distant horizon. The sky lit up bright orange. For a second or two, it was just like daylight had returned. There was an audible collective intake of breath as the flames leapt up 20, 30 feet into the air.

'The oil depot,' said Abu-Kamal. 'They blew it up – the oil depot.'

Fire engines with sirens screaming and lights flashing raced in one direction or another.

Radio Baghdad continued broadcasting, well after its normal signing off time. There were messages of support from regional leaders and army generals. One or two tribal leaders gave their allegiance to the new regime. Fidel Castro, still fighting in the mountains of Cuba, sent his congratulations and support, but the British government expressed concern, as did the USA. The Soviet Union kept its options open.

Ministers, judges, police chiefs, the head of *al-Mukhabarat*, and those associated with the old regime were rounded up and taken into custody, except for the biggest name of all, the notorious, most feared and most loathed, Prime Minister Nuri al-Said. He was the person most associated with the repressive regime, whose services were enlisted every time there was a need for a crackdown. He was still at large, and everyone was searching for him.

'If they don't find him soon, the old fox will leg it to Jordan. Then, the British will recognize him as the legitimate government and bring him back with an army,' said Abu-Kamal, in the grave tones of someone with long memories of the perfidious machinations of the great powers.

It was early in the morning. A lone soldier, with his rifle slung over his right shoulder, stood in the corner of Al-Jami'a Street and Nadhim Street, in the wealthy Karrada district of Baghdad. A woman wearing the traditional abaya, one or two sizes too small for her bulky body, and too long for her short stature, and with a full-face niqab, approached him. She asked for directions to Abu-Musa's residence. The voice was surprisingly low pitched. The soldier, who came from the poor district of Al-Kadhimiya, had no idea; his job was to prevent criminals, thieves or agent provocateurs from taking advantage of the confusion to break into homes or shops, to loot and steal.

'What street does Abu-Musa live on, do you know?' she repeated.

'No,' came the reply. '*Ummi*, you shouldn't be out at this time, go home,' said the soldier.

The woman turned around and, as she did, the bottom of her abaya swayed. Her shiny left shoe became visible. It was only a flash, but it was unmistakable; a black leather shoe, size twelve, a man's shoe. The soldier's pulse galloped like an Arabian horse on a desert mission, his mouth dried up, and there was a sudden rush of adrenaline through his veins. He inhaled deeply, and it took a moment before his training kicked in. He lifted the rifle from his shoulder, loaded it, stood upright and pointed it at the woman, and shouted, '*Halt!*' and, for no other reason than a well-rehearsed drill, added, '*Name and number!*'

The 'woman' stopped, turned around, and slowly lifted her face covering. A familiar face, a feared face, looked back at the soldier.

An authoritative voice, the voice of someone used to issuing orders, and who expects them to be obeyed, calmly said, 'Put the gun down, soldier.'

It was as if time slowed down to allow his brain to process the images and thoughts that were racing around inside his head; conflicting images, contrasting thoughts, including his poor mother in bed with tuberculosis who couldn't afford penicillin, his father working nights in a bakery never earning enough to feed the family, his school days, his ambitions, his dreams, his loyalty to the King, the national anthem in praise of the King that he sang with others every morning in the school yard. But the image that kept coming into his head, repeatedly, was of police officers beating up a young man in the street, in front of his house. It was rumoured that he had complained about the rise in the price of tomatoes to Ahmed Al-Halaq, the barber, who ran his business from a high chair on the pavement with a mirror leaning against a lamp post, and who spent more time talking to customers and passers-by than cutting hair. They took turns punching that young man in the guts – thud, thud, THUD, THUD.

'You know who I am?' said Nuri Al-Said. 'I represent the King. What you are doing is treason, so put the gun down, and you're in for a very big reward...'

...thud, thud, THUD, THUD.

It is not unknown for history to place the fate of a nation in the hands of the most unexpected and exceptionally ordinary individual. The success or failure of the revolution, the future of the country, was literally in the hands of this lone soldier – to be precise, in the index finger of his right hand gently caressing the trigger of the rifle which he held firmly against his right shoulder.

'*The King is dead*,' he whispered.

The familiar face, the feared face, continued to move towards him. 'The King is dead,' repeated the soldier. '*THE KING IS DEAD*.'

The blood started to drain from Nuri Al-Said's familiar, feared face. It turned pale, and looked frightened, pathetic, almost pitiful. He diminished in size, looked weak, vulnerable and, above all, comical, in an abaya that was gradually shifting off his left shoulder.

THUD, THUD, THUD, THUD.

The soldier pulled the trigger.

BANG.

Nuri Al-Said fell back, crumpled and collapsed in a heap of women's clothes.

'This is how the mighty fall,' mused the soldier.

The soldier was calm. This was not an impulse shooting, it was deliberate.

The gunshot startled his commanding officer, who ran over, and upon seeing Nuri Al-Said on the ground bleeding, not dead, unclipped his holster, pulled out his Beretta revolver, removed the safety lock, and shot the iconic figure of the ancient regime in the head, twice.

Other soldiers and officers gathered around. They started shooting in the air in celebration. Soldiers in the next neighbourhood joined them, and others further away did the same. And so it spread, right across the capital.

'He is dead,' said Abu-Kamal, when the sound of gunfire reached Rosette's house. 'He's been caught and killed.'

It took half an hour before an announcement was made on the radio.

It was not an ordinary mob, a mindless mob, with pillage and plunder on its mind. This was a mob with a difference. They didn't break into houses, they didn't rob shops, and they didn't frighten old women in the streets. If anything, old women came out to cheer them on. It was a question of punishment to fit the crime; a bullet in the head, a quick death, did not seem to fit the crime. Ordinary individuals, unrelated and unknown to each other, from different parts of the capital, spontaneously marched to the morgue where the body of Nuri al-Said was kept. They seized it and took it on a macabre procession, a state funeral of sorts. There was no coffin and no horse-drawn carriage. People lined the streets, not to pay their respect, but their disrespect; there were crowds, but they were not mourning, they were celebrating. Some looked on, some clapped, some chanted, others sang, and women ululated. Some spat on his body, others kicked it, kids threw stones, and a few helped pull it along. Most called the name of a loved one, a son, a daughter, a wife, or a father, as they chastised the corpse. A taxi driver drove his car over the crumbling corpse, twice.

The mob changed in size, as it trod the streets of Baghdad, but numbered never less than 500, as some drifted away, having done what seemed to be their duty to avenge those that had been tortured and killed. Many others joined in.

The mob had no leadership, but it was disciplined, like a group of ants carrying a large green leaf, taking turns in lifting it and moving it along to its destination. Except, in this case, there was no destination, as oblivion awaited the corpse. There was to be no resting place for the mutilated body, and its remains were burned at sunset, with no trace left.

A man with a solemn face and a large grey moustache, whose stoop belied his relatively young age of thirty-five, wearing the traditional headdress and a long white robe with a walking stick, pushed his way through the crowd; not to witness the demise of the most hated man in the country, but to chew a piece of his flesh. The solemn-faced man departed without saying a word. Everyone understood, everyone empathized.

Everyone had a tale to tell.

It was savage, the savagery of a lion that had been kept in a cage, continually poked with a stick, tortured and humiliated, on a daily basis. Having noticed the gate unlatched and unguarded, such a beast would leap out, rise majestically up onto its hind legs and, with a glorious roar, lunge into its tormentor. And so, what happened was beastly, it was brutal, it was gory, but at the same time it was natural, it was magnificent.

In the same way that seeds buried under desert sands come to life in a breath-taking array of dazzling colours and aromas when rain finally arrives, the revolution released the hopes, aspirations and talents of the people into extraordinary political and social change. Trades unions sprung up, political parties emerged, bookshops and book stalls popped up everywhere, newspapers were launched, rallies and meetings were held. Women were encouraged to throw away their abayas and their hijabs and embrace the new age of liberation.

Nigret al-Salman prison closed and the political prisoners were released. Among them was Heskel Kojaman. When he was released, after nine years in prison, Heskel had no family or relations left in Iraq, and the Communist Party shunned and abandoned him.

19

2003 – Willesden Green, North West London

'The Central Committee of the Communist Party wanted Jewish communist prisoners to become Muslims, on the grounds that, since religion doesn't matter, you might as well be a Muslim as a Jew. Problem solved,' said Heskel, sitting at the kitchen table in his house in North West London. Next to him sat his wife, Habiba. A carer made tea for Farouk, who had come to visit. Heskel spoke with difficulty, but coherently. He was eighty-two.

'To my surprise,' he continued, 'some of my closest friends that were in prison with me, went along with it. I wouldn't. I said this does not solve a problem, it only condones and perpetuates it. It was Hitler who talked about Jews being a problem.'

He coughed and sipped some tea.

'The twenty-odd years I was in the Party didn't seem to count,' he continued. 'They wouldn't provide surety for me to come out. You see, political prisoners were released immediately after the July revolution, but Jewish political prisoners had to have a guarantor before they were let out. They left me high and dry. Close friends, long-time comrades, wouldn't talk to me.'

* * *

Heskel found it difficult to get a job. The Jews wouldn't employ him, because he was a communist, and the Muslims wouldn't, because he was a Jew. He had few people he could call on, but one of them was Um-Kamal.

Heskel was made very welcome at Um-Kamal's home. 'You must stay for dinner,' she would say, when he came to visit. Had the revolution been a year earlier, her son, Sasson, would have been released, and she would have had him at home with her. Heskel was the nearest she could get to him. Heskel would tell her stories about Sasson – what he did, how he spent his time in prison, the games they played, the books they read; anecdotes which she loved to listen to, and which Heskel repeated every time he came to her house. He spared her the gory details, the cruel and inhumane treatment, the beatings, the isolation, the lack of food and water, the torture, and the massacre in Kut.

When the police raided Heskel's house, they arrested everyone who happened to be there – his wife, Habiba, her friend who had stayed overnight, his seventy-year-old mother, his two brothers, and his uncle who was visiting. On the same day, Habiba's sixteen-year-old brother, her sister and her aunt were also arrested. All in all, ten of Heskel's relatives were taken.

His wife and mother were taken to the women's prison. They didn't see Heskel again, until he arrived in Israel twelve years later.

* * *

'THE BEATINGS AND torture started immediately we got to the headquarters of *al-Mukhabarat*. After beating me with truncheons and kicking me in the guts, I was left hanging upside down, with my hands tied up for a whole night,' recalled Heskel.

'Did you admit to being a member of the Communist Party?' asked Farouk.

'No, of course not. A confession would not help. If anything, you'd get a harsher sentence. The rule was never to admit to anything. They didn't need confessions to send you to prison. Anyone's word would do; a man in the street, a passer-by, people who didn't know you, anyone.'

'Did anyone confess under torture?' asked Farouk.

'One or two did, and turned into informers. One gave *al-Mukhabarat* documents with names and addresses. That's how they were able to round up so many of us.'

'I was moved to Abu Ghraib prison, and stayed in solitary, in a dungeon with no light, till my trial, sleeping on cold concrete floors. I was there for a month.'

Farouk turned the Dictaphone on and pressed REC.

'There were about twenty of us in the court at the same time, five of them relatives of mine. The trial lasted two days. They asked us our names and addresses, and read out the charges: conspiring to overthrow the government, membership of a banned organization, or disrespecting the King, and so on.'

* * *

Twenty prisoners were squeezed into two rows, with armed guards at each end, and several policemen scattered around the semi-circular court. The lights were dim, apart from on the elevated, large oak desk, which had two large table lamps on each side. The prisoners were nudged with rifle butts to stand, as the civilian judge flanked by two military men entered the courtroom and plunged themselves into the three leather armchairs behind the desk.

'I declare this session of the Baghdad martial court open,' shouted the judge, as he banged a wooden gavel on the desk.

* * *

THERE WERE NO lawyers, and we had no right to question the witnesses, no way of defending ourselves. At the end, the judge retired and came back with his sentences. The Jews got harsher sentences, between seven and ten years. Non-Jews got between five and seven years.

'So many people were arrested, the court was sitting day and night, sometimes till early in the morning. Everyone was found guilty; the minimum sentence for a man was three years; women got off lightly with sentences ranging from two to five years.'

'Did Sasson tell you what happened when he was sentenced?'

'No, he didn't,' replied Heskel. 'It is the same story for everyone. It wasn't as if there was a trial. The sentence you got depended on who the judge was.'

'Kamal was arrested with Sasson,' said Farouk, 'but he wasn't charged. Sasson got eight years, and Kamal went free.'

'I didn't know that. How did that happen?'

'That's what I'm trying to find out.'

'Did Abu-Kamal bribe the judge?'

'I doubt it,' said Farouk, 'because we didn't have that sort of money. In any case, why only Kamal?'

'Did Sasson tell you anything?'

'No, he didn't. We never talked about families. It only depresses you.'

Farouk took a sip of tea from the delicate porcelain tea cup. 'I came to visit Sasson in prison, more than once.'

'Did you? Who did you come with?'

'My mother,' said Farouk. 'Sa'id and Layla came as well.'

'Did you go to Nigret al-Salman?'

'Of course,' said Farouk. 'I remember the long journey through the desert. What amazed me was how happy and joyful the prisoners were. Some with iron shackles around their ankles were still joking and laughing.'

'Of course! What else could we do? We had to for the sake of our families.'

'You were my heroes.'

Heskel deliberated for a while and said, 'Heroes! No. We weren't heroes, we were inside, couldn't do anything. The heroes were the people outside.' After a pause, he added, 'Historians glorify the dead, the martyrs. But history is made by the living, not the dead.'

20

1958 – Prophet Nahum's miracle

THE ROAD TO the Tomb of Nahum was rough and bumpy. The taxi, an old American Buick, had seen better days. The passengers felt every stone and bump, let alone the frequent potholes and occasional rock that the smooth tyres transmitted to their bones, courtesy of the rusty suspension. At certain speeds, on some stretches of the long road from Aqrah, where the sequence of bumps coincided with the natural resonant frequency of the suspension of the Buick, this resulted in the car wobbling up and down in a cycle of alarmingly increasing highs and lows. The driver accelerated to avoid the suspension breaking into pieces, as the car was forced to reach such heights that the subsequent descent could have snapped the suspension.

The villagers saw the car coming a long way off before it arrived. They were on a mountain, and they could see the road stretching way out into the flat plain.

They didn't see many visitors to this secluded part of Kurdistan, so they gathered to meet the car. When they realized that it was the doctor from Aqrah, the village police chief and the judge came out to welcome him.

The village housed the ancient shrine of a Jewish prophet by the name of Nahum, which dates back to around 600BC and lies at Alqosh, a small pretty village on the slopes of Alqosh Mountain in Nineveh province. The tomb had been neglected since Jewish Kurds had left Iraq en masse. Um-Kamal, originally from that part of the country, had always wanted to visit the shrine. Her son, Kamal, woke up one Saturday morning, and decided, on an impulse, to close the clinic and take her there.

'I'll take you to the shrine,' said the Chief of Police, when he learned of the purpose of their visit. 'But first, you must rest and have a drink and a little to eat.'

'You must come to my home,' interjected the judge, to the obvious irritation of the Chief of Police. Then, pointing to a young man who was standing a few yards away, the judge shouted, 'Hey, you, Ghulam, go and tell Um-Hussain to get ready to receive the doctor and his mother. Go on, quickly.' The young man took off the rifle that was resting on his left shoulder, held it in his right hand, and, without an instant of thought or hesitation, took off in the manner of a dog obeying an order from his master.

'We don't get any visitors anymore,' explained the police chief, as he brushed the dust off his immaculately pressed grey uniform and straightened his pointed moustache. 'Not long ago, we had thousands coming to visit the shrine – Jews… pilgrims… bringing their families and their money. It was like a big festival.'

'But don't worry,' said the judge, 'the tomb is well looked after by the Christian priest. He promised Rabbi Kakhunna that he would look after it, and he's kept his promise. It's part of our cultural heritage, and we're proud of it.'

'Here,' said the Chief of Police, as he helped Um-Kamal navigate the obstructions that littered the road, 'we live happily with each other. We are not barbarians; we don't go around killing each other.'

The 'little to eat' turned out to be a feast, with a spread of hot, flat bread, straight from the *tannour*, goat's cheese, hard-boiled shelled eggs, a goat skin full of fresh milk, and succulent red watermelons sliced into boat-shaped segments studded with black seeds that added to its ecstatic appeal. There were peaches and plums, and open pomegranates, showing their bright scarlet-red seeds, sparkled in the sun rays that managed to seep through the small gaps left uncovered by the shutters of the judge's mansion. Thin green cucumbers bent to form a semi-circle, and there was a variety of nuts and dry-roasted pumpkin seeds. But there was no meat; everything was kosher, all laid out on a large red and brown blanket on the floor. An electric fan hummed in the corner, turning now to the left, now to the right, and back again. Kamal took a central place, surrounded by the other men. Um-Kamal sat with the women, in an adjoining room.

Not long after they settled down to eat and talk, about anything and nothing, voices were heard coming from the entrance hall to the prosperous mansion, built in the style of a Venetian palace.

'What is the commotion?' asked the judge, as he swallowed a piece of goat's cheese and a slice of melon. A servant with bowed head, his body bent, forming a right-angle that made the upper part of his body almost horizontal with the floor, walked over gingerly and whispered into the judge's ear.

'What? *El-Duktor* is not here to see patients. He is here on a pilgrimage!' replied the judge.

'I don't mind. I'm here, so I might as well–' began Kamal, hoping to escape the idle chatter and do something useful.

'No question,' said the judge. 'Send them away.'

'Really, it's all right. I brought my bag with me, just in case.'

The judge relented. 'Okay, but let *el-Duktor* finish his lunch first.'

The servant withdrew, in the manner he had entered, with head bowed and an almost horizontal upper body.

After a glass of dark red, sweet chai, the judge took Kamal into what looked like a storeroom. The room was dark. A young man in his twenties sat on a stool holding a shepherd's crook in his right hand, staring into space. An older man, with shabby clothes and a face that told of the severity of life for the poor in these semi-feudal tribal communities, held the young man's left hand. As soon as he saw Kamal enter, the old man walked towards him, bent down on his knees, and kissed his hand.

'No need for that,' said Kamal.

The old man took no notice. His life experience had taught him that when his betters said 'no need', they didn't mean it. He kissed Kamal's other hand.

'Get up, stand up. I'm here to help you.'

The judge rebuked the old man in Kurdish, 'Tell *el-Duktor* what is wrong. Don't waste his time.'

'Please, may Allah bless you and give you many sons,' began the old man.

'Speak in Arabic,' barked the judge. 'What's the matter with you? Speak in Arabic to *el-Duktor*.'

'It's all right,' said Kamal, in Kurdish, 'tell me what is wrong.'

'I didn't know you spoke Kurdish *Duktor*,' said the judge.

'Only a little.'

'Bless you, bless you,' the old man said, still on his knees. He continued, 'It's not me. I'd rather die. I'm an old man, and I only have few years to live. No, no, it's my son, Anwar.'

The old man walked back to where the young man sat, and put his trembling right arm gently around his son's shoulders.

'Tell us what is so important that *el-Duktor* had to be interrupted when he's here on a pilgrimage?' said the judge.

'You see *Duktor*,' pointing to his son's eyes, 'my son can't see. He's blind.' The old man's voice broke, then he composed himself. 'He is the breadwinner, our only son, the only breadwinner in the family.'

Kamal was puzzled. What was he expected to do, cure the blind?

'Was he born that way?' asked Kamal.

'Of course he was,' interrupted the judge. 'He's wasting your time, *Duktor*.'

'Oh no, no. He took the goats for grazing, and when he came back his eyes were blank, empty. He couldn't see, he was blind. They say it's Allah's will. We'll starve without him. This is not the will of Allah! It isn't, is it, *Duktor?*'

'What do you expect *el-Duktor* to do?' intervened the judge. Then, turning to Kamal and speaking in Arabic, he said, 'These shepherds, they are all the same, ignorant. Ignorant and filthy, they are always asking for something. You should see the people I get in my court. Most probably he had too much Arak, fell on his head, and lost his sight. And,' he added in Kurdish, 'he has no money to pay you for your troubles.'

'Your Excellency, I have money. I have savings.'

'This will cost you at least 3 dinars. You don't have this sort of money, do you?'

'Your son is a shepherd, you said?' asked Kamal, in Kurdish.

'Yes, yes, bless you *Duktor*, bless you.'

'How long has he been a shepherd?'

'All his life. He went out grazing the goats at the age of twelve. One day here, one day there. And now he goes away for one, two, three weeks at a time. He's a good shepherd and a good son. The Pasha trusts him, and lets him take the sheep away.'

'Tell me what happened.'

'Speak,' shouted the judge. 'Tell *el-Duktor* what happened, we haven't got all day.'

'Yes, yes, your Excellency. *Duktor*, he took the goats to the other side of Alqosh Mountain. It's a long way, but the grazing is good there. He was away for four weeks. He had a good tent and looked after himself well. He's a good shepherd, he is.'

'And then, what happened?' asked Kamal.

'Well, when he came back, he said to Um-Anwar, his mother, that he couldn't see very well, that everything seemed to be hazy and when he woke up the next day, he couldn't see anything. Not his mother, not his sister, nothing.'

'When did this take place?'

'On Thursday, two days ago.'

Kamal went over to the young man, who continued to sit motionless, staring into space, saying nothing.

'Anwar, how do you feel?'

'He is very well. He's strong, but he can't see anything,' the old man answered.

'Did you fall recently? Did you hit your head?'

'No, he didn't. He is a good son, law-abiding, and he doesn't drink.'

'Can't your son speak?'

'He hasn't said a word since he lost his sight. He just sits and stares, in a trance.'

Kamal took the young man's temperature and felt his pulse.

'It's too dark in here. Can we go outside?'

The blind young man, staring straight ahead into space, moved his crook to the left, then to the right, and in doing so he caught the back of the judge's foot. The judge swore and moved towards the young man to scold him. The young man, unaware of the situation, stood up and stumbled into the oncoming judge's arms.

The judge pushed him sharply away and brushed his silk waistcoat, in the manner of someone brushing away a piece of excrement. The young man fell back on the stool, which crumpled, and he ended up on the floor. The old man quickly moved between him and the judge, who was preparing to kick the helpless, blind young man.

'Sorry, sorry your Excellency, sorry. Please, forgive him. He didn't mean to hit you; he didn't do it on purpose. He can't see, you see? He can't see.'

He then started to brush the judge's waistcoat, but the judge pushed him away, saying, 'Keep your filthy hands off me, you filthy dogs,' and following Kamal out.

A servant opened the main door, and Kamal, the young man guided by his father, and the disgruntled judge stepped out into the bright midday sun.

Kamal put his right hand on the young man's left eye and examined his right eye. He repeated the procedure for the right eye. He then separated the eyelids of the left eye and inspected the tissue underneath. He examined the pupil for size. The pupil was dilated, and he repeated the procedure for the right eye, with similar satisfactory results. Throughout, the old man held his son's hand as a gesture of assurance and support.

'Follow my finger,' Kamal instructed the young man, as he moved his index finger to the first position of the eight cardinal directions. There was no response from the young man.

'Of course, you can't see my finger,' mused Kamal in Arabic.

'Move your eye to top left.'

The young man moved his head to the top left.

'No, no, keep your head steady, and move your eyes... now left... bottom left. Good. Now, top. Good. Top right. Good. Right... and bottom right.'

The old man's anxiety began to fade a little due to what he thought were encouraging remarks from the doctor.

They went back inside. Kamal had to do something, give him something, if only to show that he cared. He put his hand in his bag and picked up a bottle of vitamins that he had not used for a long time – vitamins A and B.

'Take these, two a day,' said Kamal to the young man. The old man took the bottle of capsules with genuine, though exaggerated, gratitude.

'*Duktor*, I don't have 3 dinars.'

'How much do you have? What can you afford?'

'*Duktor!*' interrupted the judge, who, speaking in Arabic, went on, 'You can't do that. He must pay you properly. It'll only encourage them to expect to get things for nothing.'

At that moment, Um-Kamal, who was becoming increasingly concerned by the raised voices that reached the women's room, where the judge's wife was entertaining her and other women guests, came into the storeroom. She just caught the last few words of the judge.

Kamal spoke in Arabic to her.

A shiver went down Um-Kamal's spine as she listened. For a little while, she said nothing.

She gasped. 'This is the prophet's work,' she told her son. 'Prophet Nahum arranged for you to save this man's sight. It's a sign. You mustn't take any money from him, not a single fils. The prophet is testing you, so make it a gift to Nahum.'

Kamal smiled. The old man looked puzzled, as he couldn't understand a word of what was being said. The young man continued to look straight into space. The judge raised his eyebrows in disbelief.

'Um-Kamal, my mother, says this is the prophet's work, Prophet Nahum.' Kamal addressed the bewildered old man in Kurdish. 'She says I mustn't take any money from you. It's free. Consider it a gift from the prophet.'

'Thank you, bless you, may Allah bless you with a good wife with strong hips to give you ten boys, healthy boys, good boys, like my son.' He went back to the young man, and prepared to leave.

The young man got up and walked straight to Um-Kamal, who was standing at the main entrance. With his eyes wide open, he looked into hers. He could not see, but he looked deep into her soul, and said, in a quiet voice that was meant for her and her alone, 'Good fortune awaits you. Allah will bless you in his own way.'

Um-Kamal looked back at him. She did not see his face, she only saw Prophet Nahum's. She was stunned, transfixed, her limbs went weak, and she couldn't speak. She inhaled, but did not exhale and, although Kurdish was not a language she spoke, she understood every word the young man said. Before she recovered, the young man, holding his shepherd's crook in his right hand and the old man's shoulder with the other, disappeared through the main door. The door closed.

The large green iron door was opened by the young priest with a large rusty key selected from among others that were knotted to a long chain slung over his shoulder. There were early signs of neglect when Um-Kamal and her son stepped through the archway at the entrance to the shrine of Prophet Nahum, escorted by the young priest from the local church. 'We try to look after it as much as we can,' said the priest, 'but we need money to do that.'

The inside walkways leading to the tomb were littered with debris and masonry that had fallen out of the walls and archways.

The staircase, leading to what were the living quarters which once housed the pilgrims, had collapsed in on itself, leaving a heap of stones and rubble.

Um-Kamal was walking in front, eager to get to the tomb. She suddenly stopped. In front of her was a long rectangular box, Nahum's sarcophagus, partially hidden behind a faded green, spiral themed gate, with strips of old cloth from previous pilgrimages knotted to it. This was the legendary Tomb of Nahum. There were faded Hebrew writings on the wall, plaques, candelabras and lanterns smothered with thick layers of dust, and a blanket of complex formations of cobwebs, under a partially collapsed roof.

The young priest took another large key from the long chain he carried over his shoulder and unlocked the large padlock. He pushed hard, whereupon the gate reluctantly opened, rotating slowly on its rusty hinges to reveal the interred remains of the prophet.

Um-Kamal went in first and placed her hand over the faded green cloth covering the sarcophagus. Head bowed, she recited a prayer in Hebrew, picked up a stone, and placed it against the shrine. Under the stone, she placed 5 dinars.

Kamal stood at the entrance to the tomb. Men and women were not allowed to be in the shrine at the same time. Um-Kamal came out, exhausted. She looked as if she had just had an out-of-body experience.

Kamal entered the shrine. There was nothing much to look at, just a grave: a large box covered with a shabby green cloth. Gone was the green calico cloth, gone was the crown that sat on it, gone was the glitter of candelabras, and gone were the Persian carpets that had once covered the floor. Yet, Kamal was overawed. The idea of the remains of someone who had lived thousands of years ago being there, inside a box, was fascinating. Kamal closed his eyes and felt history, 3,000 years of history, travel through his bones. Historic as well as recent personal events, some of which he was not able to discern, rushed through him like a storm. It was overwhelming. This was not a religious experience, and it was not a spiritual experience. It was a physical, personal experience, similar to that experienced by astrophysicists when they receive signals from way back in time, a fraction of a second after the birth of the universe. This was the kind of experience that makes one reassess humanity's place in the universe, recalibrate one's place in the world, and come to the realization of one's insignificance in a non-ending space-time continuum on one hand, and one's significance here and now on the other.

The sense of something old and enduring coming to an end overwhelmed Kamal, as he stood motionless, looking at what was once the grand tomb of a prophet, which now lay in ruins. Tears began to flow down his face, as he began to cry. He was crying for himself.

A week later, a stranger pulling a goat by a rope tied around its slender neck, pushed his way through the busy market square in Aqrah.

'Is this goat for sale?' asked the butcher.

'No, it's a gift,' replied the stranger.

'A gift to the Pasha?' asked the butcher.

'No, *el-Duktor*,' said the stranger.

'*El-Duktor?*' exclaimed a turbaned man sipping tea.

'Yes, *el-Duktor*. *El-Duktor* saved my nephew. He brought back his sight,' said the stranger.

'What did he say?' asked someone.

'*El-Duktor* cured his blind nephew!' replied the man sipping tea.

'He cures the blind?' asked a woman who happened to be within earshot of the conversation.

The stranger walked up the path to the clinic, followed by a handful of children, some with bare feet, in the hope of something more interesting than hanging around in the market square throwing stones. They made a small procession up the side of the mountain with the goat, a magnificent specimen, snow white, except for a brown smudge on its long nose, ears perking attentively, and two short spiky horns.

The man shoved the goat into the clinic. The waiting room was packed. The goat pushed through, stepping on several toes. There was pushing and shoving. Words were exchanged.

Kamal looked out of the consulting room to see what the commotion was all about.

The goat owner pulled the rope sharply, squeezing the goat's neck, causing the animal to lose its footing and stumble into one or two of the patients.

The man approached Kamal.

Speaking in Kurdish, he said, '*Duktor*, may Allah bless you and your family, may Allah give you all you ask for. Bless you, bless you. This is for you.'

Kamal looked puzzled.

'You saved my nephew, Anwar. It was a miracle, a miracle. I don't know what you did, but he can see again, my nephew can see. His mother can't stop crying, she is so happy. His father wants you to have it. He couldn't make the journey, so he asked me to bring it. It is the best one he has. You won't find a better goat in the whole of Kurdistan.'

Some patients nodded; others made comments. An animated conversation began.

Kamal hesitated. 'What would I do with a goat?' he said.

The man's demeanour changed. His lips closed tightly and his face went red.

'*Duktor!* I've walked all the way from Alqosh to bring you this.'

Everyone stopped talking and looked at Kamal.

Abu-Rahman approached Kamal and, speaking in Arabic, whispered, '*Duktor*, this man has walked for two days to come here. You cannot refuse a gift. It is a great insult if you do. These are proud people. He may slash the goat's throat, or even his own throat, here and now, if you don't accept.'

'*Shukran*, thank you, *shukran*. It is very kind of you and thank your brother,' said Kamal.

The man smiled broadly, showing dark brown teeth, and, handing the rope to Kamal, he turned to the waiting patients and said triumphantly, 'He likes it, *el-Duktor* likes the goat.'

Kamal stretched out his hand and took the rope. The goat instinctively moved in the direction of the rope.

'See, *Duktor*. It likes you. The goat likes you *Duktor*.'

The waiting patients stood and clapped. The children peeping through the window also clapped.

'This is the best goat I've ever seen – such a beautiful creature,' said Kamal. He handed the rope to Abu-Rahman, who, with the satisfied expression of a cat anticipating a large bowl of cream, guided the animal to the back of the clinic.

Um-Kamal, who had been watching from the lounge, spoke in Arabic. 'I told you it was Prophet Nahum's work.'

Being a doctor, Kamal was constitutionally unable to accept a divine provenance for this miracle cure. 'There must be a natural explanation for this,' thought Kamal. And there was.

'The eye has two types of vision sensors called photoreceptors,' Kamal would later explain, as he recalled his adventures in Aqrah. 'Rods and cones are inside the retina. The rods are responsible for black and white vision. Vitamin A is usually found in animal fat. You don't get it if you don't eat fish for example. This guy is a shepherd, he lives in the wild, in open fields, there is no meat or fish; his diet lacks Vitamin A. So the rods and cones stopped working. The amazing thing is that, once you get Vitamin A, they regenerate within just eight hours. That's why he could see the very next morning.'

It was later that evening that Kamal confided his fears for the future to his mother – not just his own future, but that of his younger siblings.

'The revolution notwithstanding, the children have no future in Iraq,' he said. 'What are they going to do when they finish school? Elias is due to leave school in a few months. Do you think he will get a place at Baghdad University? I hear he wants to study civil engineering. How is he going to do that? His friends are making arrangements to go abroad, to England, America and Canada.'

His mother nodded.

'I've saved a lot of money,' continued Kamal. 'Enough to send everyone to university abroad. They can have it.'

'But we can't take all your money–'

'No, not all the money,' interrupted Kamal, 'just the money I've saved until January 22.'

Later, when she flicked the black Bakelite light switch to turn off the lonely, dim 60-watt bulb – limp at the end of a fabric-insulated wire hanging in the middle of the ceiling, and made dimmer by the scaling down of the voltage by the electricity generating board each evening at nine – and lay down on a hard cotton-filled mattress on her metal-framed bed, it dawned on her. A shiver went down her spine, followed by severe pain in the lower part of the back of her skull. For a moment, she couldn't breathe. She began to weep, quietly. January 22 was the date that Sasson had been released from prison.

21

Baghdad International Airport

KAMAL WAS RIGHT, thought Um-Kamal. They had no future in Iraq, and they had to leave. Her heart was full of fear for her sons' safety; how will they cope in a foreign land? How will they manage? They will not be short of money; Kamal had made sure of that; but at such a young age.

Earlier that year, she had seen Sa'id off, then her eldest son, Kamal. Before that, Ezra had gone and then Sasson left from that very same airport. Today it was the turn of her youngest son, Farouk.

All her sons had left Iraq. Would she ever see them again? She had a sinking feeling that she wouldn't. Only her two daughters remained with her. The family had been hollowed out, and Um-Kamal was devastated, her stomach churning, her heart beating; but she wouldn't show it. She had to stay strong.

Farouk, like his brothers, was in a hurry to go through the departure barrier. He spoke very little, and avoided eye contact. She hugged him, held him in her arms, and didn't want to let go. He was embarrassed, as that was the first time she had hugged him that way. He wriggled out, looked away and picked up his heavy suitcase which the family had spent the best part of the previous night packing and unpacking to fit in as much as possible in the one suitcase he was allowed to take without exceeding the weight limit. The airport was small, so you could see the plane on the tarmac, hear the engine whirring and the propellers turning, and see the people waving you off. You could see everything. He was so young, so vulnerable, so excited to get on a plane, standing there waiting to board.

Farouk was conscious that his mother was looking at him, waiting for him to turn around and wave a final goodbye – but he didn't; he couldn't; for had he done so, had he had a last look, he would have lost control and been unable to hold back the tears.

Um-Kamal watched as he walked the short distance onto the tarmac to the steel staircase and then disappeared into the white and green flying machine. That might be the last time she saw him. Her heart wrenched, her eyes drowned in tears, she held her daughter Layla's hand, but she did not speak. Layla did not speak either. They saw the plane with a light on its green tail, turning alternately red then blue, take off and fly into the pale blue sky on the way to London. They watched as the plane made a right turn and disappeared into the haze of the sky. That was it. They left the airport in the taxi that was waiting for them. Not a word was spoken during the long journey back. Happy thoughts interacted with sad feelings; happy in the knowledge that her son was safe, and sad that she might not set her eyes on him again.

22

Ten years on

'We are leaving,' said Rosette.

'What do you mean, "leaving"?' asked Um-Kamal.

'Leaving Iraq, early in the morning.'

It was 1970.

Murad had just heard from Abu-Salman that they were to be ready to leave the very next day, at four in the morning, before sunrise. It had been three weeks since Abu-Salman, a wheeler dealer with extensive contacts with Jews and Muslims, many with unsavoury reputations, agreed to make arrangements for the family to flee.

'Bring a small bag each, the essentials only, nothing else, otherwise suspicions will be raised. You can also bring a suitcase, just one suitcase.'

Rosette, her husband, their two children, ten-year-old Ruben and five-year-old Gracie, together with Um-Kamal and Abu-Kamal, were to take the more dangerous route to Iran via Kurdistan. The safer option, crossing Shatt al-Arab in the south, was no longer feasible. Tension between the two neighbouring countries had escalated, with their armies confronting each other along the shores of the famous waterway.

Life had changed since Abd al-Karim Qasim was brutally murdered in a military coup by Ba'athist officers, bringing to an end what many Jews regarded as their golden age in modern Iraq, when restrictions on Jews had been lifted, passports had been issued, and businesses had thrived. It was during that exceptional period that Layla completed a degree in chemistry at the Baghdad University and, soon after, went to do a PhD at the National Institute for Medical Research in Mill Hill in London.

In the years that followed the end of Qasim's regime, thousands were arrested, communists were hunted and murdered, and hundreds were hanged. The Jews fared worse than most, with a campaign of vilification in the press and on radio. They were branded Zionists, conspirators, working for Israel through an extensive web of spying networks. On one single day, fourteen people were hanged, twelve of them Jews. They were left in the main square to rot.

Murad himself was arrested. He had been observed working late one night in his doctor's practice, and that was enough to accuse him of conspiring with the British to overthrow the government. He spent eleven days in a prison cell with twelve others, sleeping on a bare concrete floor with their jackets and shoes for pillows. To lift their spirits, each had to tell a story or talk about something, anything that came to mind. Murad was lucky. Unlike the others in his cell, who got long prison sentences, Murad was released. It was Abu-Salman's work. He arranged for a hefty bribe to be paid to a high-ranking officer in *al-Mukhabarat*.

It was this personal experience that prompted Rosette to tell her husband that they must flee the country. They kept their plans secret from Um-Kamal and Abu-Kamal, as well as from their two children.

'I need to go and buy a large, strong suitcase,' Murad said to his wife who, with Um-Kamal, was sifting through their belongings to pick out the items to take in light of the restriction of one case for the whole family. To avoid raising suspicions, Murad went in the middle of the day, when the sun was at its peak and the streets deserted. He drove the car to a side street and parked it around the corner. He then proceeded to Rashid Street, which was empty but for a military truck and a couple of soldiers. He was crossing the street to get to Abu-Salim's leather shop, when the two soldiers grabbed him and bundled him into the military truck. He tried to reason with them, but they were not interested.

He squatted on the hot metal floor. The air was hot and dry. 'This is surely the end,' he thought. 'They don't need to hang me. An hour of this and I'll suffocate.' He wondered if their house had been raided. Suddenly, another man, dressed in the traditional dishdasha, was thrown into the truck, followed by a third and a fourth. Murad recognized one of them.

'Abu-Mansoor?'

'*Duktor? Duktor* Murad?'

'Yes, yes. What's going on?'

'You crossed the road in the wrong place.'

'What do you mean, the wrong place?'

'You didn't use the crossing.'

'What crossing?'

'The new white stripes on the road, what do they call it? *Hammer wahshi?* Zebra, zebra crossing. They are arresting anyone who is not using it.'

'Is this a new law?' asked Murad.

'Who knows?'

'What do we do?'

'Those soldiers only want to make some money, and who can blame them?' said Abu-Mansoor. 'A quarter dinar will do it.'

'Here,' said Murad, putting his hand in the inside pocket of his jacket. 'Give them a dinar. Just get me out.'

They let them out and Murad returned home.

'Where is the suitcase?' asked Rosette.

'It's a long story,' said Murad.

It was 4AM the next day. The family was ready. The house was dark, and the lights were off. They sat waiting in the large lounge of Rosette's house in the prosperous district of Karrada. Sparkie, the much-loved King Charles spaniel, lay curled in Gracie's lap. With the exception of jewellery and a substantial amount of cash, they were leaving everything behind: the furniture, the beds and bedding, the wardrobes, the Danish oak dining table and chairs, the Bush television-radio-gramophone console and the Persian carpets. Murad carried his family's cash in a leather money belt tied to his waist. Abu-Kamal carried the little he had in his jacket pocket. The house was to be left in the manner of a family going on holiday.

'If anyone asks,' Murad told his young children, 'we are going on holiday for a couple of weeks to Sersink.'

There was a faint knock on the door. The dog barked. Gracie pacified him. It was Abu-Salman. He gave Murad a folded piece of paper.

'Go to this address, it's a garage. The owner, Abdul-Malik, is expecting you. A taxi will take you to Erbil.'

'What about the car?'

'Leave it with Abdul-Malik. He gets to keep it.'

Murad picked up the bulging old suitcase, walked to the door and, looking at Abu-Salman, said, 'Look after the dog.'

'Don't worry, I will,' said Abu-Salman.

'It's no time to worry about a dog,' said Abu-Kamal.

Gracie was last to leave. She put Sparkie in the hallway. 'Stay there, there's a good boy.'

Sparkie whimpered. 'Goodbye,' she whispered.

Rosette pulled her by the hand, and closed the door behind her.

They put the suitcase in the boot, and quietly stepped into the family Pontiac, with Murad in the driving seat.

The road to Erbil was long and, apart from army trucks and the occasional Russian-built lorry, empty. It majestically cut through the plains of upper Mesopotamia, the area between the Tigris and the Euphrates, known as Al-Jazirah or 'island', towards the hills and mountains of Kurdistan. The sun rose on their right, its pink rays throwing long shadows on the roadside. The driver kept his right foot firmly on the accelerator, pressing it as far as it would go, and kept it there regardless of the state of the road or oncoming traffic. He chain-smoked his way to their destination, saying very little, but cursing every time he had to swerve to avoid a pothole. He saved his more elaborate language for the more substantial potholes.

The journey was pleasant enough for the travellers to enjoy the vast expanse of the mostly arid landscape. Abu-Kamal looked back through the rear window and saw Mesopotamia disappearing behind him. The black tarmac stretched out by the speeding car was like his guts being pulled out and laid down along the land of his ancestors. He felt a knot in his stomach. Um-Kamal held the two youngsters in her arms, close to her chest.

Murad tried to engage the driver in conversation, without success. 'It must be the smugglers' code of silence,' whispered Rosette. She placed her hand over his. There was more than a hint of nervous trembling.

For the two children, the journey was almost an adventure. They passed signs pointing to places they read about, regions they had heard of, and city names they saw printed on maps. They were intrigued by the vastness of the country, its serenity and its sheer beauty.

'Look! Look! This is Kirkuk's oil field,' said Ruben, pointing out the distant flames emerging from a huge pipe stretching high above the landscape. 'They say it lights up the sky at night, just like a sun.' Above them, in the clear sky, a phalanx of white storks flew in the distinctive V-formation of migratory birds.

The driver lifted his foot off the accelerator and the car began to slow down. They were approaching a checkpoint. Before the car came to a stop, a lone sentry had a quick glance and waved them on. There was a collective sigh of relief.

Soon after this, the driver started to slow the car again. They were approaching a second checkpoint. This time, a more alert sentry demanded that the car come to a full stop. Um-Kamal pulled her abaya firmly around her shoulders and pulled the niqab over her face. The two children crouched, trying to make themselves invisible.

'*El-Duktor* and his family are going to Sersink... on holiday,' explained the driver.

The sentry walked around to the other side of the taxi, where Murad was sitting. Murad immediately volunteered, '*Duktor* Murad,' lifting his ID card up to show the sentry. The sentry immediately saluted, as he would a superior officer. The driver pressed the accelerator, and the car screeched away.

The third checkpoint was more elaborate, more like a road block than a checkpoint, manned by an army officer with a handgun in a holster on his right hip and two soldiers. The driver got out and started an animated conversation with the officer. A sinking feeling of dread and fear descended upon the occupants of the car. The two soldiers stood at either side. There was menace in the air.

Rosette nudged Murad, urging him to get out. He did. He stretched out his arm to shake hands with the officer. The officer took no notice.

'Murad, *Duktor* Murad,' he said.

The officer examined Murad's identity card.

'*Duktor*, where are you going?'

'*Wallah*, I promise, Captain, we're going on holiday–'

'*Mulazim Awwal*, First Lieutenant,' interrupted the officer, pointing to the two stars on his shoulder.

'*Mulazim, Mulazim Awwal*, Lieutenant, Captain. I'm taking the family to Sersink.' Pointing to Um-Kamal and her husband at the back of the car, he continued, 'The in-laws, Um-Kamal and Abu-Kamal, Allah bless them, *maridhin*, they are sick; Baghdad's heat is not good for them, they need the fresh, cool mountain air.'

The lieutenant was unimpressed.

'Open the boot.'

'Yes, sir. Of course, sir,' said the driver, nodding his head several times.

The officer gestured to his minions to inspect the boot. They obediently trotted over. The driver released the car boot door with his key. It flew open, grazing the cheek bone of one of the soldiers.

'What is in the case?' asked the lieutenant; and, before Murad could answer, he said, 'Open it.'

Murad unfastened the straps, and carefully opened the case.

'*Mulazim Awwal*, Captain, it's only shirts, dresses, clothes, that's all, for the children.'

The lieutenant looked into the car. Rosette smiled. Abu-Kamal looked straight ahead. Um-Kamal pulled her abaya tighter, and the two young children sank into the black leather seat.

'You can go,' said the lieutenant, with a reluctant tone; and, for no apparent reason, he added, 'But be careful next time.'

It was late morning when the taxi driver stopped outside a drab café-cum-doss house on the outskirts of Erbil. They were taken to a room at the back, with a single window looking over an empty backyard. The barking of several dogs could be heard.

'You'll stay here till we arrange transport,' said a man in his fifties, with a thick beard and a moustache to match. The man, who didn't introduce himself, said, 'Stay low. Do not leave this room, and do not look out of the window.'

The room was large with a number of straw mats piled up in the corner. There were also three straw-seat chairs, a small table, and a bowl with a large water jug. Some light managed to penetrate the layers of dust-turned-into-mud that stained the window pane. The only other source of light came from a lonely low-watt lamp dangling from the ceiling. It was a far cry from their comfortable spacious five-bedroom house that boasted a lavish garden, a garage and two luxury bathrooms.

Um-Kamal immediately began to tidy the place up, and Rosette attended to her son and daughter. The two men, Murad and Abu-Kamal, stood in silence in the middle of the room, looking at the rotting wooden beams holding up the white-washed ceiling and the bare brick walls. The door suddenly opened. A woman in a rough-textured abaya stepped into the room, dumped a tray she was holding onto the bare floor and, without making eye contact, retreated, shutting the door behind her. Not a word was exchanged.

The two children, who had had nothing to eat or drink since they left their house early that morning, immediately tore a chunk of goat's cheese and stuffed it inside a pita, together with a wedge of cucumber. They were about to take an almighty bite, when Murad shouted, 'Don't behave like savages.'

They froze. They'd never heard their father shout at them like that before.

'They are only children,' said Um-Kamal.

'They are hungry,' said Rosette. 'Here, here, sit here and eat,' she said, pointing to the chairs.

The next day, early in the morning, the bearded man opened the door and gestured to Murad to come out. When they were out, the bearded man closed the door and said, 'Your transport is coming tomorrow.'

Murad nodded.

'It costs 300 dinars.'

'300?'

'Each.'

'But I've already paid…'

'It's for the transport.'

'What? Another 1,800 dinars?'

'Yes, transport doesn't come cheap.'

'That's extortion. You expect me to pay that?'

'If you don't pay, there will be no transport.'

When Murad went back into the room, he was trembling. His face was pale.

'What is it? What did he want?' asked Rosette.

'He wants 1,800 dinars.'

'But I thought you paid up front,' said Abu-Kamal.

'I have. I told him, I said I'm not paying again.'

Murad paused. 'I'm not paying… I'm not paying…'

He clenched his fists, his face went red, and his body started shaking.

'ONE THOUSAND AND EIGHT HUNDRED… this is what I paid Abu-Salman. What sort of people are these? They're trying to destroy me… Why is God punishing me? They have been paid and they want more… more… What else will they want from me? They might as well rip my heart out? Rip my heart…'

He began to beat his chest alternately with his left and right fists.

Rosette, Um-Kamal and Abu-Kamal spoke over each other.

'Calm down!' said Um-Kamal. 'You'll do yourself an injury.'

'Take a deep breath,' said Rosette. She held his right hand and repeated, 'Deep breath… deep breath…'

'*Murad, ibni*, my son, what will you have us do?' said Abu-Kamal. 'Stay here? Go back? What?'

'You have to pay him,' said Um-Kamal.

'Nana is right,' said Rosette.

'I'll give you the little we have,' said Abu-Kamal.

'It's only money,' said Rosette. 'It's not as if we don't have it.'

'For the sake of the children,' said Um-Kamal, 'pay him.'

The children looked up in horror.

'What's going to happen to us, Baba?' asked a nervous Ruben.

'Are they going to send us back?' asked Gracie. She ran into her mother's arms.

There was then an unintentional pause – the kind of pause that occurs when a group of people, facing a life-or-death situation, is paralysed because the one among them in whose hands lies their salvation is rendered inert by a psychological breakdown.

Knowing glances were exchanged.

Um-Kamal broke the silence.

'I have money, I'll pay.' Looking at the two frightened faces of Ruben and Gracie, she said, 'Don't be frightened my pets, don't be scared. It's going to be all right, I promise.'

Um-Kamal looked at her husband and repeated, 'I'll give him the money.'

Um-Kamal picked up her abaya, turned it inside out, and proceeded to unpick tiny stitches to reveal a pouch. Inside the pouch, neatly tied with a red ribbon, was a pile of notes.

'Here,' she said, handing the stack of notes to Murad. 'Here is 1,800 dinars.' In response to her husband's puzzled look, she explained, 'Kamal gave it to me the night before he left… for emergencies, that's what he said… 1,800 dinars… for emergencies… One… thousand… and… how did he know–'

She stopped in mid-sentence. She froze, gazing at the far corner of the room. Looking back at her was a shepherd with a crook in his hand. He was blind. Goose pimples flooded her body. Her lips moved, but no sound came out. The blind shepherd smiled. A shiver climbed up her spine. She felt light-headed.

'Are you okay?' asked Rosette. 'You look as if you've seen a ghost.'

'I have,' Um-Kamal whispered.

Everyone turned their gaze to the far corner of the room. There was nothing to see.

The next day, late in the evening, when the two youngsters were preparing to spend a third night in that godforsaken place, the door swung open. The man with the thick beard appeared.

'Come, come. Your transport is here. Hurry, hurry...'

It was a jeep this time, a Willys four-wheel-drive.

The driver, a Kurdish man in Western clothes, looked around nervously. 'Quick, inside, quickly.'

'What about the suitcase?' asked Abu-Kamal.

'Don't worry about that. We'll bring it later. Get in, get in.'

They never set eyes on the suitcase again.

The road to the Iranian border soon gave way to a rough mountain track that cut through thick forest. There was no moon that night. It was dark, and with the jeep's headlights turned off, for fear of attracting unwanted attention, it was like driving into a deep cave. The outlines of the track became visible only milliseconds before the jeep's front wheels were upon them. The driver ploughed on regardless, constantly changing gears as he took one sharp turn after another, zig-zagging up and down steep mountain slopes. Ruben and Gracie buried their heads in their grandmother's bosom. Abu-Kamal put his arms around his wife, murmuring a prayer in Hebrew. Murad and his wife, sitting in front, wondered whether taking this dangerous route was such a good idea.

At a particularly sharp turn, the driver turned the wheel sharply to the left, and the back of the jeep skidded to the right. The driver hit the brakes, and the right rear wheel left the track and was rotating freely at great speed. The car came to an abrupt stop, with its chassis resting on the edge of a ravine.

'Mummy,' cried Gracie. 'Nana,' screamed Ruben. The driver swore. Murad yelled, 'You'll kill us!' Rosette cried out, 'Careful!' and an uncharacteristic swear word escaped Abu-Kamal's lips, as Um-Kamal tightened her grip on the two children.

After a terrifying second, with Allah invoked repeatedly, everything went quiet. The only sound came from the suspended wheel gradually coming to a halt, and a collection of stones came trundling down the side of the ravine towards the deep valley below.

Abu-Kamal instinctively pressed the car door handle to get out. The car swayed, and more stones left the cliff edge.

'Don't move!' cried the driver.

He put the gear in neutral, started the engine, pressed the clutch, and slid the gears into first. He slowly released the clutch, which began to bite, and the suspended back wheel began to spin. He pressed the accelerator. The suspended wheel started spinning freely at speed. With the two front wheels unable to get a grip of the ground, they began to slip and screech. The rear-left back wheel had a better grip, and it began to skid, shifting the front of the car to the right, and so leaving the jeep in a more precarious position than before. The driver quickly turned off the engine. 'We are getting no traction,' he said.

'We'd better get out then, before the car goes over,' said Murad.

'If you do that, the car will definitely go down and take us with it.'

'What are you saying?'

The driver was calm. He spoke with authority, in the manner of someone who had faced a similar predicament before.

'The front wheels are not getting any traction,' he repeated, 'no grip; there is a lot of weight at the back. If the children could move to the front, here, with us…'

'Gracie! Come over, come and sit with us,' said Rosette.

'Are you mad?' said Murad. 'The car is precariously balanced as it is.'

'No! Murad, it makes sense,' said Rosette. Turning around, she said, 'Gracie, you first.'

'I don't want to die,' said Gracie.

'It'll be all right, I promise. Nothing will happen to you. Come and sit in my lap.'

'Slowly, don't make sudden movements,' said the driver.

Gracie pushed herself up, the car tilted a little, and more stones found their way down the slope. Gracie froze.

'Keep moving, gently, no sudden movements,' said the driver.

Gracie crept forward and squeezed herself through the gap between the two front seats, avoiding the long gear stick, and climbed into her mother's lap. Rosette squeezed her tightly and kissed her on the forehead.

Ruben followed his sister. He chose to dive, head first, over the gear stick, hitting Abu-Kamal's chin with his left foot in the process. The jeep swung dangerously. More stones were heard hurtling down into the ravine. Ruben sat on his father's knee.

The driver started the engine. Apart from the free wheel rotating furiously, the car did not budge.

'It's no good,' said the driver.

'I told you, he's going to kill us,' cried Murad.

'We need the old couple to come to the front,' said the driver.

'Are you joking? They can't,' said Rosette. 'The children only just made it.'

'I told you,' said Murad.

'It's okay,' said Um-Kamal, 'we can do it.'

Um-Kamal urged her husband forward. He pushed himself up, and immediately fell back. The jeep tilted a few degrees one way, and then the other, like a weight balance attempting to find its rest position. More stones and earth were dislodged from the cliff edge.

'Stop!' said the driver. 'Stop!'

'I said...' said Murad.

'If they move forward...' said Rosette.

'Yeah, that might do it, Allah willing, it might work,' said the driver.

'*Yallah* Abu-Kamal,' said Um-Kamal. '*Yallah*.'

The grandparents stretched out their arms, held the top of the front seats with their hands, and pulled themselves forward. Rosette and Murad pushed their children towards the windscreen. There was a perceptible tilt in the desired direction. The driver quickly pushed the ignition button, the engine spluttered into life, he pushed the gear stick forward and slowly released the clutch. The suspended wheel turned furiously and the front wheels skidded. The car began to shift forward, as the free-wheeling wheel made contact with something solid. It stopped spinning, prompting the car to bounce up and land with all its four wheels on the track, inches away from the edge. There was a collective intake of breath, followed by a collective scream. The driver pulled the hand break.

'*Allahu Akbar*,' cried the driver. Murad praised his version of Allah, as did Um-Kamal and Abu-Kamal.

A rock was heard trundling down, making a big splash as it hit the fast-flowing stream at the bottom. A hush followed. The occupants of the jeep sat very still, mouths half open, unable to process what had just happened. They didn't know whether to laugh or cry.

A barn owl splintered the stillness of the forest with a series of piercing tunes. The occupants looked at each other, and burst out laughing.

It wasn't long after that that the driver brought the jeep to a halt.

'This is as far as I go,' he announced.

They got out. They looked around. They couldn't see anything. They couldn't see anything, because there was nothing to see. They were in a small clearing surrounded by tall trees. The track had come to an end, and the jeep could go no further. Murad looked at his luminous-dial Omega watch. It was 2:32 in the morning.

'Wait here,' said the driver, as he manoeuvred the jeep around and drove off. The sound of the engine slowly faded as the jeep disappeared into the darkness of the forest, and with it went the little that remained of their hopes. Their spirits had hit rock bottom.

'What is going to happen?' asked Ruben.

'I don't know *ibni*, I don't know, son,' said Murad.

Gracie looked up, her face full of fear.

'Don't worry my little babies. Don't worry,' intervened Rosette. 'Someone will come soon.'

They stood in silence; their senses heightened. The smallest ruffle of the leaves made them turn towards whence the sound came.

'What is that?' whispered Abu-Kamal.

'*Al-dhib!* A bear!' said Um-Kamal.

'Don't be silly,' said Rosette. 'You'll only frighten the children.'

'*Al-dhib?*' screamed Gracie, and she folded herself into her mother's arms.

'It's more than one *dhib*,' said Abu-Kamal.

They waited in silent apprehension, as the sound of feet, paws, and hooves pressing on dry twigs and parched vegetation got louder and louder, and the beasts nearer and nearer.

It was at this moment that Um-Kamal felt drowsy, and her legs buckled. She collapsed and fainted. Rosette rushed to her side. She laid her flat on her back and felt her pulse. Murad opened his doctor's bag and, feeling with his hands, took out a small syringe which he gave to Rosette to hold. He repeated the process again, but couldn't find what he was looking for.

'Where is it?'

'Look in the side pocket at the front,' said Rosette.

He did. He took out a vial and looked at its label.

'What does it say?' asked Rosette.

'Can't tell. Oh, what the hell,' said Murad and, dispensing with sterilization rules, he inserted the syringe needle into the rubber top of the vial, sucked its contents into the syringe, lifted it out, stabbed it through the abaya into Um-Kamal's left thigh, and emptied its contents into her body. Everyone looked at Um-Kamal.

'Nana is dead,' whispered Gracie.

Um-Kamal stirred. She opened her eyes and made some noises. She was trying to say something.

'Don't speak, don't stress yourself, stay–' said Rosette.

'Looook!' Um-Kamal gasped, lifting her head up slightly and shifting her eyebrows in the same direction.

Rosette looked back. Murad looked back. Abu-Kamal looked back. The children looked back. Four pairs of eyes looked back at them.

The bear turned out to be a man in a Kurdish outfit, pulling two mules and a donkey with a rope that he held in his right hand.

He spoke only Kurdish. They spoke no Kurdish. After a few attempts at communication, with some words repeated several times in louder voices in the hope that that would make them more intelligible to someone who had no knowledge of the language, they resorted to the age-old communication techniques of hand movements and gestures.

The Kurdish guide, who never gave his name, walked in front. Behind him, a disgruntled mule carried Murad and the two children, followed by Um-Kamal and her daughter on the back of an equally disgruntled beast, with Abu-Kamal on the donkey at the rear. After two hours of trekking through rough terrain, they suddenly came across Haji Omran, a small, featureless village that was made almost invisible in the darkness of the night. They were exhausted. They fell asleep in their clothes, immediately after they laid on the beds that their hosts had prepared for them.

It was well into the morning when they woke up. The sun was halfway up in the southern sky. Their new hosts were friendly and hospitable and, in contrast to the smugglers they encountered earlier, couldn't stop talking. Although she didn't speak Kurdish, Um-Kamal struck a chord with the lady of the house who, it so happened, had a son named Kamal, so she was also called Um-Kamal, to everyone's delight.

After a bath and a change of clothes they were treated to a lavish lunch.

Soon after, a young female soldier, immaculately dressed in fatigues, holding a Kalashnikov rifle and wearing the insignia of the Barzani Kurdish army, the Peshmerga, came in and, speaking in English, said, 'I'm here to take you over the border.'

'What did she say?' asked Um-Kamal.

'She said she will take us to the border,' said Abu-Kamal.

'But she is a woman.'

Gracie looked in awe at the handsome, confident, young girl in army uniform with her long hair covered with an exquisite red beret.

They gathered the few belongings they had, and when they were about to step out of the door, Abu-Kamal said, 'Um-Kamal, you forgot your abaya.'

'No, I haven't,' she said. 'I haven't.'

Um-Kamal walked out. There was a spring in her step. She welcomed the embrace of the fresh mountain breeze on her un-cocooned body. As she stood in the dirt road that dissected the village, she felt as if a weight, heavier than her abaya, had been lifted.

Scantily dressed children, with bright happy faces and bare feet, followed them to the outskirts of the village. The path narrowed into a simple trek as the forest started to close in. The soldier was sure footed and seemed to know where she was going. After an hour of solid walking, the forest opened up a little.

'Here we are,' said the soldier. She pointed to a weather-worn pole, whose red paint had long faded, resting on two posts dug into the ground on each side of the track. 'This is the border.' A guard sat on a wooden box with a rifle on his lap.

Smiling broadly, and pointing to one side of the barrier and then the other, she said, 'Iraq, Iran; Iran, Iraq.'

The binary nature of her light-hearted remark carried with it a sense of finality, a point of no return.

The guard stood up. He lifted the barrier arm. The way was clear, the road was open, and the last obstacle had been lifted.

Um-Kamal stopped, and looked back. Abu-Kamal also stopped, and looked back. There was no way back. Um-Kamal nudged her husband forward, and said, '*Yallah, yallah* – soon you'll be with your sons.'

They took a few steps onto the barren, rough ground to cross the invisible threshold into another world.

A welcome party awaited them when they arrived at a small Iranian village, a mile or so from the border.

'In the name of his Excellency the Shah,' declared a smiling district chief of police to the bewildered Jewish family, 'I welcome you to the state of Iran. Welcome! Welcome!'

They were taken to what looked like a community hall where other Iraqi Jews gathered, some of whom, until recently, had been neighbours of theirs. They sat exchanging stories of their journeys. Each family had its own unique tale to tell – the horrors they encountered, the risks they took, the near-death experiences they had faced, and the obstacles they overcame.

Two official-looking men – one tall, clean shaven, 6-foot-something, and another balding, 5-foot-something, and wearing spectacles, both dressed in Western clothes – entered. Looking around, they walked towards Um-Kamal's family.

Without introducing himself, the 6-foot-something one addressed Murad. 'Welcome, how was your journey?'

'Frightening for the children and exhausting for the grandparents,' began Murad, who was eager to tell someone of their ordeal, and the heroic part he played in guiding the family to safety. 'It was a nightmare, I had to–' Murad looked tearful.

'You're here now. All of *that* is behind you.'

Murad took an instant dislike to him. He thought he was disrespectful, showing little interest in what they had been through. His pronunciation of 'Iraq' did little to endear him either. In common with all non-Arabic speaking Israeli officials, he pronounced the 'R' in 'Iraq' the way the French pronounce their 'R's', adding a 'KH' at the end, much like someone trying to spit when there is nothing to spit out. This was in an arrogant assumption that that was the way it was pronounced in Arabic.

The 6-footer had little time to waste. With his companion taking careful notes, he began.

'What is your name? Age? Profession? Which synagogue? You don't go to a synagogue? Why? Your wife's maiden name… your children's names… ages…? Do you have relatives in Israel? Their names… where do they live… their phone numbers…?'

When he had finished with Murad, he proceeded to question Abu-Kamal. When the questioning came to an end, the bald-headed one spoke.

'We have a nice hotel in Tehran, the Commodore, where you will stay and, when your papers arrive, you'll fly to Israel.'

'It will cost you nothing,' said the 6-footer. 'The Jewish Agency takes care of everything.'

The two men exchanged a few words, in a language that none of the family recognized, and walked to the middle of the hall. There was an instant hush.

'I have good news for you,' announced the bald-headed one. 'The coach will be here soon, maybe tomorrow.'

And with that, the two men left the way they came.

True to their word, the coach did arrive mid-morning the next day. Um-Kamal's family and the other refugees quickly gathered their belongings and boarded it.

The journey to Tehran was long, but pleasant, the scenery stunning, the coach comfortable, and the atmosphere tense with anticipation. The man sitting in front of Abu-Kamal was exhilarated, banging on the side of the coach and singing. Abu-Kamal was crying.

The next morning, the family gathered at the busy dining room of the Commodore Hotel for breakfast. A very large photograph of a smiling Shah in military uniform adorned the main wall. On the opposite side, there was an extensive buffet offering a comprehensive range of Jewish Iraqi food – *geymer*, boiled eggs and fried aubergine slices, fresh yogurt, melon, and hot *samoon*.

After breakfast, Rosette leaned over to her parents and said, 'We are moving out of the hotel.'

'Moving out?' said Abu-Kamal.

'Yes.'

'When?'

'Today.'

'Today!' said Um-Kamal.

'Murad has booked a room in a hotel nearby.'

'Why?' asked Abu-Kamal. 'It's nice here.'

'It *is* a nice hotel,' said Rosette.

'But that will cost you. You'll have to pay,' said Abu-Kamal.

'Yes, we will.'

'So, why are you going?'

'Abu-Kamal,' said Murad, 'Father, do you think the Jewish Agency is paying all this money out of the goodness of their heart? They expect you to go to Israel, to live there.'

'We are; that's what we are going to do. No?'

'We are not; we don't want to live in Israel.'

'We've been thinking about it for a long time,' said Rosette.

'You never said,' said Um-Kamal.

'We didn't want to worry you,' said Rosette.

'We have decided to go to Canada,' said Murad.

'Can we go to London?' asked Ruben.

'Yes, London!' echoed Gracie.

'We'll stop in London on the way,' said Rosette.

'What about us?' asked Abu-Kamal.

'Come with us,' said Rosette. 'Why don't you come with us?'

For a second the idea of going to England appealed to Abu-Kamal. He had fond memories of the English from when he served in the British army, way back during the First World War.

'What? Go to a foreign country? Not knowing the language? Not knowing anyone?' said Um-Kamal.

'It's not for us,' said Abu-Kamal.

'We are doing this for the children,' said Murad. Pointing to Ruben and Gracie, he added, 'For you two, the apples of my eye and the lights of my life.'

'What future will they have in Israel?' said Rosette. 'Soon there'll be another war.'

'They'll end up in the army. They will have to fight, shoot people, shoot Muslims,' said Murad. 'This is not the life we want for them.'

'We want a new start for them,' said Rosette.

'A new start for all of us,' said Murad.

Um-Kamal bit her lip. For her, life had always been a sequence of mixed fortunes. She was happy; soon she would be reunited with her beloved Sasson and his older brother, Ezra. She was also sad. She was parting with her two grandchildren. She was there at their birth and she had looked after them ever since. Abu-Kamal's emotions, faced with this unexpected turn of events, could not be discerned. His face was as inscrutable as always.

'I tell you what,' said Rosette, looking at her two children. 'Let's go shopping. We need to buy a lot of things.'

23

Rosette, Toronto

'I THOUGHT NANA was dead. I couldn't feel any pulse, but Murad was very quick,' said Rosette. 'He injected her with adrenalin, and she woke up.'

'He saved her life?'

'Yes, he saved her life.'

Farouk moved the Dictaphone closer to Rosette. They were sitting in his sister's spacious five-bedroom, double-garage house in Toronto. Farouk took advantage of Murad having been called out to see a patient to talk to Rosette. Murad had an unedifying habit of not knowing when not to be involved.

'We asked them, Baba and Nana; we asked them to come with us, but they wouldn't.'

'I'm not surprised. They have no one here, and it's cold,' said Farouk.

'They came to visit. Baba was not happy that I chose not to continue practising medicine. He said: "You're a doctor, what are you doing spending your time in the kitchen?" He thought Murad put pressure on me.'

'Did he?'

'No. It just wasn't possible. You see, the medical qualification we have is not recognized in Canada. To get a licence to practise involves attending courses, residency training, and several exams. It took a year for Murad to get his licence. We had Ruben and Gracie.

They had no friends here, they spoke little English, and they were starting a new school. There was no way we could both do it.'

'Baba was very proud of you,' said Farouk. 'You must have been one of the few women to study medicine in Iraq.'

'Yes, but I was the first woman from a poor district like Qamber Ali. Most parents didn't send their children to school, and, if they did, it was the boys. Girls never stood a chance. There were very few schools for girls. They were expected to stay at home, help with the chores, find a husband and have babies.'

'But you didn't.'

'Help with the chores? Yes, I did. I helped with household chores, looked after the children that Nana kept having, every eighteen months, like a conveyor – one child every eighteen months on the dot. But I also went to school. Baba insisted. He was very keen that I should go to school and get an education, as well as the boys.'

'It must have been very difficult,' said Farouk.

'Financially, very difficult. We barely survived. I helped as soon as I could, making dresses for girls, and Kamal got a few hours working for a relative, and Ezra did as well, when he was old enough. We gave all the money to Nana. That's how we survived.'

'I meant very difficult being Jewish and a woman at the university.'

'Not that difficult. There were Jewish students in my year. Murad was one of them, and that's how we met. Politically, it was very tense. A lot of students were arrested, many were members of the Communist Party.'

'Did you join?'

'What?'

'The Communist Party.'

'You know, I don't know why, but I never told this to anyone. Secrecy becomes a habit that you carry with you throughout your life when it is a matter of life and death. Yes, I was a member. I joined soon after I started university.'

'Really?'

'I was in the women's section.'

'Did the police harass you? Were you arrested?'

'Arrested? No. In the university, only one or two women were arrested, mostly by accident. They were in the wrong place at the wrong time, but none betrayed the Party. You see, in spite of everything, the traditional respect for women meant that we were not subjected to the same kind of torture as men.'

'But the police came to our house.'

'I wasn't at home when they came.'

'What I don't understand,' said Farouk, 'is why Sasson got such a harsh sentence. He was only sixteen!'

'He confessed. He signed a confession in the middle of the night,' sighed Rosette. 'Had he waited till the morning, he would have been freed.'

'Why?'

'Why didn't he wait?'

'No. Why did he confess?'

'I don't know,' said Rosette. 'He never talks about it.'

24

Kamal, The Bronx

'BABA TAUGHT US to be competitive. Nothing short of being first satisfied him,' said Kamal, relaxing in an armchair in his modest lounge in his terraced house in the Bronx.

'He was very passionate about education,' said Farouk.

'Sometimes, even being first was not enough,' Kamal continued. 'On one occasion, I had very high marks in some exam or another, and went directly to the synagogue where Baba was praying. He had just lost his mother. I tugged at his shawl. He took his eyes off the prayer book and looked down at me.

'"I'm first in class," I said. After absorbing the information for a few seconds, he said, "That's not as important as the difference between you and the pupil who came second."

'"How many marks should that be?" I asked. "At least 10," he replied.

'When I told him it was 50, he smiled broadly, and I could see his eyes welling, and a tear sliding down his cheek. Never allowing any expression of praise to escape his lips, he brushed me off with, "Go home now, go!"

'I knew I gave him one of his happiest moments.'

'My overriding memory of you,' said Farouk, 'is hunching over a thick, heavy book reading and, from time to time, underlining some passages with a red pencil.'

Kamal's face lit up. He laughed, the sort of laugh that expresses more pleasure than merriment.

'One evening,' continued Farouk, 'to keep me quiet, you sat me on your lap while reading. The rusty old metal table lamp was so dim, you had to push the lamp shade very close to the book, so that it almost obscured the English words on the page. An aunt or niece of ours walked in and, pointing at me, said, "Isn't he clever? He can read already."

'You said, "And he understands everything." To prove it, you began to ask me questions about some medical conditions with unfathomable Latin names; the sort of questions that had the answer embedded in them, much like asking someone the colour of a red car. She was very impressed when I answered correctly.'

'It's fascinating that you should remember such a trivial thing so clearly,' said Kamal.

'I remember it like it was yesterday. I couldn't have been more than four or five, but I can picture it very clearly.'

Anne, Kamal's partner, who had been living with him ever since his acrimonious divorce, sat quietly, as she always did when Kamal went down memory lane ('It's good for him,' she would say). She stood up. 'I'm going to make some tea, do you want some?' she asked.

Kamal nodded and Farouk said yes.

'I know they were difficult times, but from the way you tell these stories, there were enjoyable times too,' said Farouk.

'Of course there were.'

'You must have been happy in Aqrah.'

'It was a mixture of contentment and anxiety,' said Kamal. 'I was content because I was achieving something, helping people, doing my job, learning, but also lonely and anxious about the future.'

'And you were very popular in the area. Didn't they sign a petition asking for you to stay when the government wanted to move you on?'

'Some people wanted to get out a petition,' said Kamal, 'but I said no. The authorities would certainly have accused me of sedition and arrested me.'

'You were arrested before Aqrah?'

'Several times,' said Kamal quietly.

'I thought it was only the once.'

'No. After I was released the first time, the police kept on harassing me. I was arrested and taken to a police station on the flimsiest of excuses, but never detained.'

'By "the first time", do you mean when you were arrested with Sasson?'

'Yes.'

'What happened?'

'They came to the medical school, and took me.'

'I thought you were arrested at home.'

'No! No! Sasson was picked up at home. I was at the university. Sasson was a member of the Communist Party and they'd found a document with my name on it. Sasson was proposing me as a candidate member of the Party. They came to the medical school, and they took me to the Central Police Station in Baghdad. There were lots of people there, all professionals, professors, lawyers, teachers, students. No criminals. They kept me in a cell with eight or ten other people. We slept on bamboo mattresses. They gave you two cans, one for food and one for urine. The toilet was an open sewer. You sat on bricks.'

Kamal stood up, walked to the window, and looked out into the backyard. It began to rain.

'We were only allowed out to a small yard at the back, for half an hour a day,' continued Kamal. 'The cell was so dark that when you went out into the sunshine, you had to close your eyes. I was there for a week, or maybe ten days, and then they said I could go. Sasson got eight years.'

'Why did they let you go?'

'They had nothing on me. They found nothing. There was nothing.'

'And Sasson?'

'Sasson signed a confession. He confessed to membership of the Communist Party.'

'But that would have been suicidal, surely.'

'Well, yes. No one ever confessed, but he did.'

'Why? It doesn't make any sense. Why?'

'I don't know.'

'Did you try to talk him out of it?'

'I couldn't.'

'But you were in the same police station. Didn't you see him?'

'No. You're kidding! No, never saw him; only at the trial.'

'Were you in front of the judge at the same time?'

'No, twenty or thirty of us waited in a small anteroom adjoining the courtroom. He went in before me.'

Anne came in with two plain white mugs. She placed them on the coffee table. Kamal leaned over, picked up the mug nearest to him and took a sip of tea, making sure it cooled down as it passed his lips by simultaneously inhaling air.

There was a pause.

Kamal half turned towards Farouk and said, 'Isn't it funny how some events leave a lasting impression, whereas others, more important ones, fade away.'

25

Sasson, Haifa

SASSON'S WIFE, SARAH, a slender, 5-foot-tall woman, with a stick, walked into the lounge with two large orange drinks on a tray, and placed each one delicately on the glass-topped coffee table.

She spoke in Hebrew. 'I thought you may like a drink. Are you still reminiscing?'

Sasson laughed. He spoke in Hebrew too. She smiled.

'She asked if we were still reminiscing,' said Sasson in English. 'I said it's not so much reminiscing as an interrogation.' He laughed again.

Farouk took little notice, too eager to continue his enquiries.

'Do you recall when you were arrested?' he asked, as soon as Sarah had left the room.

'Yes, of course. Of course I do.'

'What happened?'

'There was a raid on the Party. Hundreds were arrested. They arrested someone, and he had a document with Kamal's name on it. When they came to arrest Kamal, I was in the house, so they took me too.'

'So, they had nothing on you?'

'No, nothing. I wasn't a member of the Party,' said Sasson.

'You weren't?'

'I was sixteen. I couldn't join till I was seventeen. It was a rule that Fahd introduced. I did join later.'

'So, what was your connection with the Party?'

'I was a runner. I delivered messages, documents, leaflets. I used to carry them among my school books. Nobody suspects a school kid to be carrying leaflets. In fact, on the day the police came to our house, I had a document I was to deliver the next day to a house not too far from where we lived.'

'Did the police find it?'

'No, I had it hidden.'

'Was Kamal a member?'

'Yes, he was, but I didn't know at the time.'

'Surely you'd have known – your own brother?'

'No, not really. The Party was illegal, underground. It had a cell structure. For security, you only knew those in your own cell, five or six at most. Each cell had a leader, and all cell leaders in a district formed a district branch, with its own leader, and so on. Only senior Party members had access to the wider membership.'

'So, why did you confess?' asked Farouk. 'Were you afraid of being tortured?'

'Everyone was afraid of torture, but no one confessed. Only a few did and betrayed the Party. That's what frustrated them – the police. They couldn't get any confessions. But that wasn't the reason. Kamal said he couldn't stand being in prison, that he would kill himself at the first opportunity, so I told them that I was the member of the Party and that he had nothing to do with it.'

'You signed a confession?'

'Yes.'

'Why did they let Kamal go?' asked Farouk. 'They could have sent both of you to prison. It's not as if they needed evidence or witnesses to convict.'

'They were so pleased to obtain a clean admission. Those who confessed did so under torture, so when they came in front of a judge, they could hardly walk. They had bruises and broken bones. With me, it was like they'd struck gold. It was as if I was a justification of everything they were doing, the proof that they were right. They couldn't wait to put me in front of a judge. They were prepared to agree to anything,' said Sasson.

'But you didn't tell anyone?'

'It didn't seem necessary.'

'You never spoke about it to anyone, not even to your wife?' Farouk was incredulous.

'I didn't do it for other people.'

'You did it for Kamal!'

'No!' said Sasson sharply. 'I did it for myself.'

'You know that Kamal doesn't recall any of this?'

'Doesn't he?'

'He is adamant,' said Farouk. 'I asked him directly. He insists he wasn't in the same police cell as you, and that you never saw each other, let alone spoke.'

'He confided in Sahib, though.'

'Sahib?'

'Sahib, his friend from medical school,' said Sasson. 'Also a Jew.'

'Sahib? The one who was shot standing next to you?'

'Yeah, yeah. Sahib was arrested and sent to Kut not long before the massacre. When a new prisoner arrived, everyone wanted to talk to him to find out about their families and what was going on outside. When I told him I was Kamal's brother, he said, "I didn't realize how close the two of you were." These were his exact words.'

Sasson paused.

'When I started university in Haifa, a year or so after I arrived in Israel, Kamal was working in Manchester before he went to the United States. He sent me a cheque. I don't recall the amount, a few hundred pounds, but there was no explanation, just a cheque, with a note saying I may need the money. A month later, another cheque arrived. I sent it back and told him there was no need.'

* * *

It was 1960 when Kamal, a young registrar at Rochdale Infirmary, found a letter on the doormat of his small apartment. It had an Israeli stamp. A little chill went up his spine, for although he had left Iraq more than a year ago, the fear associated with anything to do with Israel lingered. He opened it.

The envelope contained the cheque that he had sent to Sasson.

'Any mail?' asked Jonathan, the junior doctor who shared the small apartment in the hospital complex.

'Just a letter from Israel.'

'Good news?'

'It's a cheque.'

'A cheque? That's nice.'

'No. A returned cheque.'

'From the bank?'

'No, no, my brother, Sasson, in Israel. He has returned the cheque I sent him.'

'Oh! Why?'

'Why I sent him the cheque, or why he sent it back?

'Both.'

'I sent it to help him out while he was at university.'

'And…?'

'Oh, I don't know, just a note, saying "not necessary".'

Kamal tore up the cheque, and threw it in the bin, together with the note and the envelope. He then proceeded to pour milk on the corn flakes that he already had in a bowl. He sat at the round dining table, and said, 'Are you going to the pub tonight?'

'Yes, we always do on Fridays.'

'I think I'll join you.'

'Never thought I'd see the day. All these months, and never once have you come out for a drink. What's going on?'

'I don't know, just feel like it.'

'Well, Bernie will be pleased. She keeps asking about you.'

'Bernie?'

'You know, the Irish nurse. I think she fancies you.'

'Are you trying to make me change my mind?'

They laughed.

* * *

'Why didn't you keep the money? After all, you saved him from prison – probably saved his life,' said Farouk.

'It is much better that way,' said Sasson.

'What do you mean?' asked Farouk.

'His contribution far outweighed mine. Look how he looked after his patients – a true servant of the people.'

'Is that why you confessed?' enquired Farouk. 'Because Kamal would make a better contribution in life than you?'

'No. Look, I was sixteen, I wasn't thinking deep thoughts; but now I can see it actually worked out for the better.'

'How can you say that? You spent more than nine years in prison, beaten up, tortured, terrorized…'

'Okay, okay. But it did work out in the end,' said Sasson.

'Everything works out in the end.'

'No, it doesn't. We could have been killed.'

'You almost were,' said Farouk.

'Precisely – *almost*.'

'Do you think Kamal felt guilty?'

'About what?'

'About you spending nine years in prison,' said Farouk.

'I don't know, maybe… maybe.'

'Would you do the same thing again?' asked Farouk.

Sasson paused. 'It's not easy to say. It is a process of thought. Given the same situation, with the same thought process, one could end up doing the same thing. It wasn't an accident that could be avoided. It was a process of thought – a state of mind.'

26

The Reunion, Ramat Gan

UM-KAMAL LOOKED AT her children. She was proud, very proud; three doctors, one of them a surgeon, another with a PhD in chemistry, two engineers, one mathematician and a school teacher.

'Abu-Kamal, we haven't done a bad job,' she whispered to herself, and, as was often the case, she remembered Kamila and Benjamin, and wondered what would they have become, had they lived.

It was 2005 – the first grand reunion of the whole family, except for Abu-Kamal, who had passed away three years ago. Um-Kamal and all her children with their wives, partners and children, some of whom had to fly across oceans and continents, gathered in Ramat Gan. There were long and emotional introductions.

No sooner had they all gathered than each sibling reverted to the slot in the family structure that he or she occupied back when the family lived in Qamber Ali. Imperceptibly, and effortlessly, the family dynamics that had existed then were now restored: Rosette, the eldest, full of wisdom and experience, forever careful not to upstage her husband or look cleverer than him, which of course she was. Kamal, the eldest son, much respected and held in great affection, still feeling a responsibility towards family members. Ezra with his political acumen and satirical approach to life's grim incidents. Sasson who had suffered most, but sought no sympathy, with an unassuming intelligence and high intellect. Elias, content to quietly observe proceedings, with no overwhelming compulsion to intervene. Layla, with an abundance of love, forever using the quintessentially Jewish Iraqi expression for profound empathy, '*b'dalak*'; underrated, and for a long time resented by Um-Kamal for not having been born a boy. Sa'id, considered the cleverest of them all, attracting unsolicited attention, listened to with interest, and who could do no wrong. Farouk, the youngest, much loved, in the same way a family loves a mischievous puppy – once again feeling the protective presence of his brothers and sisters. Being the youngest, Farouk was able to escape the innate pleasantries and empty exchanges that permeate the initial stages of such gatherings. His Aunt Salima, Um-Kamal's younger sister, hugged him with genuine fondness and affection. 'You only wanted to come with us when we left,' she said, with a broad smile. 'You wanted me to put you in a suitcase and take you.'

Farouk had no recollection of her, or the event.

If there had been tension or envy, it would have resurfaced. That, of course, is why many family Christmas gatherings are quarrelsome. It's not so much the alcohol as the resurrection of old feelings and emotions, and the reincarnation of past rivalries. But, in the case of Um-Kamal's family, it was anything but tense or ill-tempered. It was natural, familiarly informal and relaxed, belying the fact that the family hadn't met this way for fifty years.

The venue was the unassuming Habib's Kebab restaurant, specializing in Iraqi-style food, situated in the outskirts of Tel Aviv amid a café, a fruit and veg store and a few other retail outlets. The inside was sparse with a stone floor, bare walls and functional fluorescent lights. The only concession to aesthetics was provided by a rare Eastern Rosella parrot proudly displaying its colourful feathers on a perch inside a magnificent dome-shaped iron cage in the far corner. Its bright red tuft, and green and yellow breast, contrasted sharply with the bland, colourless walls. It provided a continuous stream of random words and an assortment of short, sharp tunes. The distinctive aroma of freshly *tannour*-baked bread mingled with the seductive smell of charcoal-grilled lamb. There was nothing to commend the place, other than the food.

It took a long time before they settled around the long table that was set up specially for the occasion, as family members exchanged pleasantries, and introduced their wives and husbands. Children suddenly found uncles, aunts and cousins they never knew existed, or they may have heard of, but never met. The three older brothers sat next to each other at the top right-hand corner, as other family members negotiated their way to be in earshot of them, in the knowledge that from that quarter would emanate the most interesting and comical recollections.

Every now and then, Ezra would lean over and relate some anecdote about when they were in Iraq that would make Kamal turn red in the face, and laugh loudly in the manner of someone trying to expel something that has taken residence in his throat. To the outsider, the recalled anecdote might be humorous, but not so funny as to reduce Kamal to tears. However, for the three brothers, it brought back some of the absurdity of the lives they had shared, and the absence of logic or reason that seemed to have punctuated everyday life in Iraq; a unique type of nostalgia, delving into the past with a comical eye, finding humour within tragedy; painful events that are intuitively filtered out through a careful selection of instances and episodes of their lives.

The laughter was infectious, and soon the rest of the family joined in as the anecdotes were repeated for their benefit. They were received with a mixture of amusement and incredulity by outsiders who generally looked on with a smile, content that others were happy. The exception was Murad, who found such outbursts childish, ungracious and irritating, especially since he wasn't at the centre of attention.

Ezra would tell the story first in Arabic, interspersed with a few English words. He would then go over it again in Hebrew, with a smattering of Arabic, repeating the punchline several times for effect in Hebrew and English, eliciting amusement from all quarters.

Stories like that of Shlomo Karadi, who was disowned by his wealthy family for falling in love with an Indian girl and ended up in the streets, distressed and deluded. He was accused of trying to blow up the iron bridge in Baghdad and sentenced to ten years. He used to count the days to his release by the number of *samoons* he would eat till then. There was the anecdote about the teacher who, instead of teaching them physics, spent all his time telling stories about the adventures he had had on land and sea, when everyone knew he never had set foot outside of Baghdad. Ezra had a rare ability to make people smile and laugh, even though he spoke a language that was alien to them. There was also the time they spent at their aunt's, when they had to leave home for fear of attacks by Muslim mobs. They couldn't eat the food because it was so greasy, so they hid it in handkerchiefs and surreptitiously threw it out of the window. There were accounts of the alleyways and narrow streets in the slums of Baghdad where they grew up, which flooded every time it rained. People had to cross the street by stepping gingerly from one stone to another to prevent their shoes getting wet or, for those who could afford it, by jumping on the back of a *hamaal* who took them across for a few fils. The streets were lit by kerosene lamps, and there was a night watchman who kept falling asleep.

When the first electric street light was installed, throngs of kids used to run and shout in celebration every time the night watchman came to switch it on with his long stick, that had a hook at the end. From the laughter, it seemed that these were happy days.

To the uninitiated, it made little sense, but to Um-Kamal's family it encapsulated the nuggets, the shiny gold nuggets, of the life they shared in Iraq; the murkier the surroundings, the greater the shine. The younger ones had fewer such memories, for they left at a younger age, but they too understood and joined in the fun.

Stacks of steamy *khubz* flat bread, fresh from the *tannour*, were placed at various spots along the table and, without any prompting, everyone dug in. Bowls of Iraqi-style salad, with tomatoes, onions and cucumber, cut into small pieces, garnished with coriander and doused in fresh lemon juice, were brought next. Then smaller bowls filled with a variety of pickled vegetables, from cauliflower and cabbage to thickly sliced carrots, arrived to supplement the feast. There were bowls of fat-stalked celery, aubergine in olive oil, and green and red peppers.

'Try this one, Elias,' urged Farouk.

'You remember this?' said Sa'id, pointing to a deep-yellow pickled mango called *amba*. 'Have some of this,' another said, pointing to a plate of garlicky, freshly prepared humus. Most couldn't resist the temptation of salad wrapped in slices of *khubz*, which was devoured with heightened enthusiasm. The more discerning kept their consumption to a minimum in anticipation of the moist and tender shish and doner kebab of lamb and chicken.

Long metal skewers were unceremoniously dumped, in bunches of five or six, alongside newly refreshed stacks of bread.

The chatter, a mixture of Hebrew, Arabic and English, was loud – made even louder by the need for translation that sometimes had to be retranslated by those who regarded themselves as having a better grasp of the language. Farouk translated Arabic to English for his wife, Valerie, sitting next to him. Sa'id did the same for his wife, Daphne. Neither Farouk nor Sa'id spoke Hebrew. They relied on Layla, who assumed the role of interpreter-in-chief, translating Hebrew to English, English to Hebrew and, where necessary, Arabic to Hebrew for Israeli-born nephews and nieces. The level of the conversation approached what would in other circumstances be regarded as shouting, but was normal by the standards of the Middle East.

As skewers were relieved of their succulent load, more were brought in by very attentive staff who, though experienced, took a surprisingly long time to understand a simple order of a bottle of red wine.

The chatter was interrupted by loud and hearty laughter from the corner, where the three brothers sat. Those in their immediate vicinity leaned over to ascertain the cause of the merriment and passed it down the table, resulting in slowly subsiding laughter as the anecdote was told several times, to people who could not really appreciate it. And so it went on.

The noise generated by the conversations, the story telling, and the reminiscing moved in waves and peaks and troughs, as the chatter from a large gathering tends to do; and, as is always the case, when the noise reaches an unexpected trough, someone, unaware of the coming drop in the level of the ambient noise, fails to adjust his or her auditory output in time to prevent a word or a phrase belting out, causing amusement or embarrassment, depending on what was inadvertently divulged. And that was what happened to Anne, whose voice suddenly and unexpectedly boomed, 'A THOUSAND DOLLARS EVERY YEAR...'

Anne, Kamal's partner, a tall Jamaican, with a naturally assertive voice, similar in tone to that of a gospel preacher, realizing she was now centre of attention, with all eyes focused upon her, was happy to explain.

'Dr A gave $1,000 to each of the three students who got the highest marks in maths, physics and science at the local high school,' she said in her normal, self-assured manner. 'He's always believed in education. He made sure that all of you,' she said, looking at Um-Kamal's younger children, 'went to university. He thought it was his duty to do so. Your father couldn't, so he gave all his money to your father for him to pass on. He even sent money to Sasson, soon after he arrived in Israel.'

The news that Kamal had sent money to Sasson was a revelation. Everyone stopped whatever they were doing. Anne looked bewildered. She thought it was common knowledge. All eyes turned to Sasson.

'Yes,' said Sasson, adding in Hebrew, 'רזחב האחמהה תא יתחלש.'

Valerie looked to her husband Farouk for translation. Hebrew and Arabic sounded the same to her. He looked at Layla sitting across the table, as did Sa'id.

'Sasson said he had sent the money back,' said Layla.

Kamal remembered the cheque coming back, with a note saying it was not necessary. He still found it strange, as he only wanted to help him through university.

'Why?' Sasson was asked. 'Your brother was trying to make it up to you.'

'What do you mean?' said Sasson.

'Making up for the evidence he gave against you!' said Murad.

A hush descended on the table.

Kamal placed a fat pumpkin seed between his teeth, cracked it, disposed of the shell, and chewed the seed. With raised eyebrows, he looked at Murad.

'Murad, Murad. You think I betrayed Sasson, my own brother?'

'Well, yes,' ventured Murad in Arabic. 'Everyone thinks so.'

Murad waited in anticipation; he had always been hugely jealous of Kamal, who outshone him in academic achievement, as well as wealth, seemingly without trying very hard and who, to his mind, should not be held in the high regard in which his wife and the rest of the family held him.

Rosette was uneasy. She looked at her mother, as if to say, 'Don't get involved.' She turned to Murad, but kept her thoughts to herself. She would never contradict her husband in public – something his vanity as the head of his family could not handle. She would, no doubt, have a few words with him later.

Um-Kamal looked at Murad with disapprobation, but bit her tongue, and, out of respect for her daughter, she said nothing.

Elias looked at Sa'id with an anxious face and whispered in English, 'That wasn't necessary.'

Ezra said something in Hebrew, to the effect of, 'Let's not go there.'

Layla, speaking in Arabic, said, 'There is no harm knowing.'

Farouk leaned over to Sa'id and said, 'Murad is not satisfied unless he's the centre of attention.'

'Putting people down makes him feel superior,' replied Sa'id.

The hush became a deafening silence. There was tension around the table, and even Um-Kamal's great grandchildren felt the gravity of the moment. They stopped their games and stared at the expectant faces of their uncles and aunts. Even the parrot paused its rendition of its favourite tune, cocked its head to the left, puffed its red tuft, and looked on with its small beak half open.

A waiter, holding a stack of skewers in his right hand, sensing the tension, hesitated before cautiously stretching his arm over the heads of Murad and Rosette, and carefully placing the steaming skewers in the middle of the table. The steaming lamb was left undisturbed.

Kamal spoke in Arabic.

Farouk provided instantaneous translation to his wife and Daphne who were sitting opposite each other. 'He said he did no such thing.'

Um-Kamal spoke in the only language she knew, Arabic. 'Murad...'

'What a thing to say, Murad,' translated Farouk.

'But I heard you say that many a time,' persisted Murad, in Arabic.

'Murad! Leave it,' said Elias, in English.

'Don't distress yourself, Elias,' said his wife, Martha. She spoke in Portuguese, before turning to Hebrew. Elias took no notice. He spoke neither Portuguese nor Hebrew.

'What did she say?' asked Farouk.

Daphne, the only person present who had a smattering of Portuguese, translated. 'She said something like, "Elias doesn't want…" no… "doesn't like to talk about these things."'

Layla translating the Hebrew part, said, 'She asked Murad to leave it and to stop creating trouble.'

The numerous conversations, all at the same time, in several languages intermingled with the obligatory translations resembled a mini General Assembly of the United Nations. Voices were raised, not in anger, but to make themselves heard above the general cacophony.

Rosette was talking to Murad, who didn't look convinced.

'It's none of our business,' was heard, in Arabic.

Um-Kamal was in conversation with her younger sister, Salima, sitting next to her.

Ezra said something to Sasson.

Anne put her hand on Kamal's forehead, as she was concerned about his blood pressure.

Farouk looked at Sa'id in exasperation. 'You have to do something,' he said.

'Yes, honey, do something,' said Daphne.

Sa'id, speaking in a delicate upmarket New York American accent, cut through the hubbub. Looking at Kamal, he said, 'Kamal, Kamal. As I understand it, when you were in the police station, Sasson was going to confess, and you persuaded him to tell the police it was only him, and that you had nothing to do with it.'

Rosette translated to her mother. Um-Kamal was perplexed. She looked directly at Sa'id. She spoke in Arabic.

'And how do you know that?' was Farouk's translation.

'No one told me; just the impression I have,' said Sa'id. He spoke in English.

Rosette translated.

Layla spoke in English. 'Why don't we find out what actually happened?'

She repeated it in Arabic, and again in Hebrew.

When Kamal spoke, it was in the manner of a doctor explaining a well-established medical condition to a patient. He spoke in Arabic.

'I never saw Sasson. They put me in a different cell. We were separated, we never had a chance to speak,' he asserted with professional finality. 'If we were able to talk, do you think I would have let him sign that confession?'

'What did he say?' asked Valerie and Daphne, almost in unison.

'He said he never saw Sasson at the police station,' translated Sa'id.

Everyone turned to look at Sasson.

Sasson looked at Farouk. Farouk looked at Sasson.

Sasson spoke in Hebrew.

Layla was taken aback, speechless.

Martha looked at her husband, with concern.

'What did he say?' asked Um-Kamal, in Arabic

'What did she say?' asked Daphne.

'She wanted to know what Sasson had said,' said Sa'id.

'What did *he* say?'

'I don't know, he spoke in Hebrew,' said Sa'id.

'I thought it was Arabic.'

'No, honey, Hebrew.'

'What's going on?' asked Valerie.

'My mother wants to know what Sasson said,' explained Farouk.

'What did he say?'

'Who?'

'Sasson.'

'He said he didn't see Kamal in the police station.'

Sa'id looked at Farouk. 'You don't know that's what Sasson said.' He turned to Layla.

Layla, having recovered her composure, spoke: 'Sasson said he doesn't know what the fuss is all about. He said they were kept in separate cells, they never had a chance to talk, and that Kamal didn't know anything about his confession.'

Sa'id turned to Farouk. 'Since when did you speak Hebrew?'

'I don't.'

'How did you know what Sasson said?'

'It's a thought process,' said Farouk, 'a state of mind.'

Um-Kamal spoke in Arabic. Farouk gave simultaneous translation.

'*Ibni*… my son, why did you confess... why did you tell them you were a member of the Party? If you had waited… for… what… "*sa'aat*"?'

'"Hours",' said Sa'id.

'If you had only waited for a few hours...' Farouk continued his translation, 'till the morning… you... both of you would have been out. I had a letter from... "*al-qadi*", "*al-qadi*"… what is "*al-qadi*"?'

'"Judge", "judge".'

'Yes, from that nice judge, well-known judge, Abu ... someone…'

Salima spoke in Arabic.

'Um-Kamal, come on, don't distress yourself Um-Kamal. You don't know if Abu-Adnan would have got your sons off.'

Um-Kamal put her hands on her cheeks, gently shook her head, and murmured, 'Why? Why? Oh, why?'

'There, there. Don't fret,' said Salima. She put her arms around Um-Kamal's shoulders and gave her a forceful hug.

'Every time I think of it, I wonder, what if…'

'What if? What if? What if both of your sons went to prison?' said Salima. 'Have you thought of that? Be grateful only one son went. It could have been two, or even three.'

'I know, I know.'

'Look at everyone, look at your children and grandchildren, look how well they've all done, look how happy they are.'

'Yes. I wish Abu-Kamal was here to see it.'

'He is here. He's here. He is looking on, and he's happy and very proud.'

'I know, I know, Salima. You're right. Let's not talk about it anymore. Let us not ruin the evening.'

The parrot punctured the air with a squawk, opened its white beak, and mimicked human voices. This made the waiters smile. The mothers who spoke Hebrew gave the children an embarrassed gaze.

The children went back to whatever children do to pass the time on occasions that are held primarily for adults.

The adults went back to their favourite activity, munching into pita bread stuffed with lamb kebab and salad.

Sa'id picked up a wine bottle and poured red wine for Daphne, Valerie and Farouk.

Kamal stretched out his arm and pulled a large chicken cube off one of the recently arrived skewers, and put it straight into his mouth. He looked at Sasson and said, 'This chicken kebab is excellent.' Sasson concurred. He took a skewer and emptied half of its contents onto his plate, and the other half onto Ezra's.

Sa'id took a sip of wine and turned to Farouk. 'So, Farouk, did you find what you were looking for?'

'What do you mean?'

'You travelled across three continents talking to everyone. Did you get what you wanted?'

'I'm not sure I know what I was looking for,' said Farouk.

'The truth?' offered Sa'id.

'The truth?'

'Yes, the truth.'

'The truth is not what it's cracked up to be,' said Farouk.

'Hmm...'

'But I did discover something.'

'And what was that?' asked Sa'id.

'Something that's more important than the truth.'
'What is that?'
'I discovered dark matter,' said Farouk.
'The dark matter that binds the universe?'
'No. The dark matter that binds us.'

Fawzi Ibrahim was born in Baghdad in 1943 into a large working-class Iraqi Jewish family. He moved to London in 1959 where he trained as an electronic engineer, a subject in which he lectured for thirty years and on which he became an internationally respected authority. He is the author of numerous books including *Television and Video Technology* (Newness 2007) and *Capitalism versus Planet Earth: An Irreconcilable Conflict* (Muswell Press 2012). A lifelong political activist and trade unionist, he was a member of the national executive of the lecturers' union NATFHE for twenty-five years and its national treasurer for nine years. He stood in the 2003 Brent East UK Parliamentary by-election as an independent anti-war candidate.

With thanks to

Project manager Jan Woolf

Editor Akan Leander

Book design Roelof Bakker